Storytimes for Two-Year-Olds

Judy Nichols

ILLUSTRATIONS BY
Lora Sears

AMERICAN LIBRARY ASSOCIATION

Chicago and London

Designed by Charles Bozett

Composed by Ampersand, Inc.
  in Itek Souvenir
  on a Digitek typesetting
  system

Printed on 50-pound Glatfelter,
  a pH-neutral stock, and bound
  in 10-point Carolina cover stock
  by Edwards Brothers, Inc.
  ∞

Library of Congress Cataloging-in-Publication Data

Nichols, Judy.
  Storytimes for two-year-olds.

  Includes bibliographies.
  1. Story-telling. 2. Libraries, Children's—
Activity programs. I. Title. II. Title: Storytimes
for two-years-olds.
Z718.3N5 1987   027.62'51   86-32151
ISBN 0-8389-0451-3

Printed in the United States of America.
93 92 91 90 89   6 5 4 3

Contents

Preface

Six years ago I faced my first storytime program for toddlers armed with the few articles available in the literature about similar programs, ten years of experience with preschool storytimes, and three months' worth of research into the needs and characteristics of this age group. I was scared stiff! And I still felt totally inadequate.

Two-year-olds (the core of the toddler group) have terrible reputations. Coworkers and parents reacted alike, "Great idea! But it'll never work." Toddlers were perceived as too unpredictable, too undisciplined, and too flighty to participate in any group activity. Parents expressed a reluctance to bring their toddlers to the library for fear that they would be disruptive, and most staff members agreed.

It became apparent, however, that some activity for very young children was needed in our community. The number of toddlers was visibly increasing, while at the same time area preschools and day care centers did not include those under three in their programs. Parents not only felt that the library was off-limits to their little ones, but also were unaware of parenting books and materials for toddlers in the library's collection.

We plunged into the program, advertising only with a poster in the library foyer. We took ten registrations for the first six-week session. After the first week, three more parents called to enroll their children. After the second week, we had over ten names on a waiting list, and over 50 people registered for the second six-week session. All without any advertising outside the library. We discovered how important this program was to both parents and children when fathers began taking days off from work to bring their toddlers when mothers could not. Vacation plans, weekly schedules, and out-of-town visitors were shuffled around the toddler storytime. After the first nervous program, we approached all others with eagerness and great expectations.

Concrete results were apparent in increased circulation statistics for picture books and parenting materials at the branch. We began to see more families in our library, even though they were not part of the program. They had heard that we offered something for very young children . . . therefore, we must have a collection to support it and the toddlers must be welcome. Overall circulation went up.

There were unexpected results as well. We discovered within a year that children entering our preschool storytime at age three were much calmer and more eager to attend than in preceding years. The instances of crying children too frightened to enter the storyspace dropped dramatically. Toddler-storytime graduates knew what to expect and what was expected of them, making preschool programs easier on the storyteller. We also had not anticipated the fierce loyalty that toddlers are capable of. Parents told us stories of being unable to drive by the library if it was closed or if they were in a hurry, for their toddler would "demand" that they stop even if there were no storytime that day. Toddlers like to talk once they master the skill, and they talked about their storytimes almost nonstop to family and friends. With publicity like that, why advertise?

We discovered we were not only entertaining the children but also that we were educating their parents. By giving parents participatory experiences in a learning environment with their children, we provided them with a role model to follow at home and an introduction to the materials they could use to help teach their children basic concepts and physical-social skills.

And they kept coming. Enrollment in preschool storytimes climbed, and repeat visits to the library continued regularly even when the children were not attending programs. Habits learned early in life can be strong ones, and parents generally will return with their children to places where the children have had positive experiences.

Whenever children's librarians gather at conferences, meetings, or informally, we talk about the programming and services we are offering and learn what other libraries are doing. By talking to other librarians who are conducting toddler storytimes, I discovered that they had all gone through the same research and trial and error processes that I had. We are each re-inventing the wheel. Many others expressed desires to offer programming for this age but did not know where to begin.

It was with these factors in mind that this book was conceived. It will present the special considerations that programming for toddlers must take into account and the materials necessary to conduct a basic program. This work will also contain suggestions for program content in the form of 33 thematic programs, suggested book titles, fingerplays, poetry, crafts, and follow-up ideas for parents and children at home.

These storytimes were developed in a new branch library with a separate program room; however, they have been conducted in one-room libraries, in meeting rooms, and in homes. The format is adaptable to many situations and with the skills and talents each individual brings to his or her own programming, it can be unique in each setting.

This work is directed toward individuals and institutions who wish to begin or to enhance existing storytime programming for toddlers. It is intended to provide a pretested format for that program, ideas and suggestions for storytime content, and encouragement to serve this age group. The resources presented here should be helpful to anyone who works with toddlers: parents, teachers, and other care-givers.

No program is solely one person's creation. I want to thank all those librarians who have been doing toddler programs for many years and who shared ideas and materials with me. My personal thanks to Greg Lubelski who provided an atmosphere of freedom and encouragement in which this program could grow; to Theresa Overwaul, Becky Arnold, Mary Lou Dwyer, and Linda Bogusch who believed and plunged into the program with energy and dedication, each adding special talents and new dimensions to it; to Nancy Renfro for her support and creativity; and to Bettina MacAyeal of ALA Publishing Services.

Acknowledgments

"Old Scarecrow Flannelboard" drawing adapted from *Storytelling with the Flannelboard,* Book 2, by Paul S. Anderson. T. S. Denison and Co., 1970. Adapted with permission of the publisher.

"Little Duck Salad" reprinted from *Celebrations: Read Aloud Holiday and Theme Book Programs,* by Caroline Feller Bauer. New York: H. W. Wilson Co., 1985. All Rights Reserved.

"Funny Potato Face" drawing adapted from *What to Do When "There's Nothing to Do."* Copyright © 1968 by the Boston Children's Medical Center. Adapted with permission of the publisher.

"Pretend Steering Wheel" and "Placemat" drawings adapted from *Purple Cow to the Rescue,* by Ann Cole, Carolyn Haas, and Betty Weinberger. Copyright © 1982 by Ann Cole, Carolyn Haas, Betty Weinberger. Illustrations copyright © 1982 by True Kelley. By permission of Little, Brown and Company.

"The Baby" and "Traffic Lights" from *Finger Frolics: Fingerplays for Young Children,* by Liz Cromwell. Copyright © 1983, Partner Press. Reprinted with permission of the author and publisher.

"Bear Straw Caddy" drawing from *Rainbows and Ice Cream: Storytimes About Things Kids Like,* by Carol Elbert and Robin Currie. Copyright © 1983 Carol Elbert, Robin Currie, Rene Lynch, and Iowa Library Association. Adapted with permission of the Iowa Library Association.

"I Shut the Door," "Kitten Is Hiding," "Make a Valentine," "Indians Are Creeping," "The Window," "Pound Goes the Hammer," and "Five Little Snowmen" from *Let's Do Fingerplays* by Marion F. Grayson. Robert B. Luce, Inc., 1962. Reprinted with permission of the publisher.

"Rabbit Cup Puppet," "Rainbow," "Frog Puppet," "Turnaround Faces," "I Know an Old Lady Sack Puppet,"

"Generic Glove Puppet," "Caterpillar/Butterfly Sock Puppet" drawings adapted from *Puppetry in Early Childhood,* by Thomas Hunt and Nancy Renfro. Courtesy Nancy Renfro Studios, Publisher.

"The Little Turtle," reprinted with permission of Macmillan Publishing Company from *Collected Poems of Vachel Lindsay.* Copyright © 1920 by Macmillan Publishing Company, renewed 1948 by Elizabeth C. Lindsay.

Adaptation of drawings "Bird Feeder" and "Paper Plate Banjo" from *How to Make SNOP Snappers and Other Fine Things,* by Robert Lopshire. Copyright © 1977 by Robert Lopshire. Adapted by permission of Greenwillow Books (A Division of William Morrow & Company).

"Busy Windshield Wipers" from *The Preschool Story Hour,* by Vardine Moore. Scarecrow Press, Inc., 1972. Metuchen, N. J. 08840. Reprinted with permission of the publisher.

"My Zipper Suit" from *Very Young Verses for Very Young Children* by Barbara Peck. Macmillan, 1941. Reprinted with permission of the publisher.

"Bears Everywhere," "Doughnut," "I Dig, Dig, Dig," "Houses," "Monkey See, Monkey Do," "Where Are the Baby Mice?", "Sometimes I Am Tall," "Boom! Bang!", "Here Is the Engine," "Wind Tricks," "Five Winds," reprinted from *Ring a Ring o' Roses: Stories, Games, and Fingerplays for Preschool Children.* Copyright © 1981, Flint, Michigan Public Library.

"Birthday Clown" drawing adapted from *Rainy Day Surprises You Can Make,* by Robyn Supraner. Courtesy of Troll Associates, Mahwah, New Jersey. Copyright Troll Associates © 1981.

Idea for Finger-Tasting Sock Puppet courtesy of the creator, Tom Tichenor.

1
Why Toddler Storytimes?

f all the age groups served by libraries and child care facilities, why should toddlers be singled out for a storytime program that takes so much planning and preparation? Who benefits from this type of program and the special considerations that need to be taken into account in offering it?

It is becoming apparent that learning occurs much earlier than previously thought. Recent studies indicate that children learn over 80 percent of the vocabulary that will serve them all their lives by the time they are five years old. Stimulation of young minds is essential to the development of intelligent adults.

Toddlers have bad reputations. We all know about "the terrible two's" with their developing independence and stubbornness and lack of social and communication skills. The transition from baby to child is feared and often compounded by well-meaning adults who are frustrated and confused by the child's behavior. They feel that little can be done except to "grin and bear it."

A storytime program for toddlers not only educates and entertains the child, but also gives parents some ideas, materials, and techniques with which to continue interaction with their children at home. This interaction in turn reinforces the storytime program and creates a feeling of trust, resourcefulness, and genuine affection for the source of the program, that is, the library.

Young, upwardly mobile parents are seeking earlier experiences outside the home for their children. In response, books, toys, and games for infants and toddlers are being marketed in ever increasing amounts. Parents may purchase books for their toddlers without considering the public library as a resource for these same items. Or they may associate the library with research, quiet reading, and fragile materials—a place not suited to noisy, active toddlers.

Libraries have been fighting this "shhh" image for a long time. Staff members in children's departments are selected because they enjoy children of all ages, and some librarians offer puzzles or toys for very young children to play with in-house or to check out. Children's collections now include board books with sturdy pages and simple illustrations appropriate for toddlers. It is important that children have some books of their own, but also that they be exposed to as many books as possible when young. Not many parents can afford to do this at today's prices.

The first indication I had that a toddler program was needed came when parents brought preschoolers (3–4-year-olds) to regular storytimes in the library. They did not want their two-year-olds to "disrupt" the library, so they would wait in the car with their younger child or make other child care arrangements. It was inconvenient for them and not always pleasant for the toddler. Both came away with negative feelings associated with the library.

After we began the parent/toddler storytime program, we not only saw more toddlers in the library but also more families coming together. No longer did one parent stay at home with the youngest member while the rest of the family visited the library to choose books. The sight of whole families in the library was pleasant to staff and library patrons alike. The library became an integral part of community life.

And who benefited? We all did. The children were provided with an opportunity to learn social skills in a group situation, broaden their worlds both physically and mentally, and be introduced to books and the library where their love of reading will grow and be nurtured.

Parents and care-givers discovered the wealth of materials available in the library for their toddlers and themselves. It was gratifying to watch them learn that their toddlers were no longer babies but capable, eager students, and that they, the parents, were the best teachers. Through participation in the storytime programs and awareness of appropriate materials for their children, many parents began using storytime techniques to turn daily routines into learning experiences for their toddlers. Some said they were also spending more time "playing and pretending" with other children in the family. They expressed delight that the storytime program acted as a support group, keeping them in contact with other parents of toddlers and making them aware of the many books on parenting in our collection.

The library also benefited in many ways. Our toddler graduates continued coming to the library to get books and to attend other library programs. Circulation increased in many categories. As parents became familiar with the collection, they chose more books for themselves and other family members. We began to see entire families using the library at times other than during scheduled programs.

Toddlers became very proprietary about the library, bringing relatives and neighbors to see where they came for storytime. This increased community exposure to library materials and services and made the library more aware of the needs of the community. A feeling of good will was generated toward the library and its staff members.

But the most important benefit was the creation of a library "habit" in both adults and children in the community. Ongoing use of the collection, services, and facility helps create a literate community where citizens will fight to support libraries, their personnel, and services.

2 Planning Considerations and Program Elements

here are many considerations when planning any kind of program, and toddler storytimes are no different. Vitally important are a clear understanding of the age level and careful audience preparation. The physical location, time of day, and program format all need to be considered.

The most crucial characteristic of toddlers is their short attention span. They distract easily; even the slightest noise or action will rob you of their attention. Don't panic! Keep in mind that a longer attention span does not develop the day before the child's third birthday. Rather, it is developed by helping the toddler to focus attention on words, objects, and actions for increasingly longer periods of time. This program was created around this primary consideration.

Other important considerations to keep in mind are:

1. Toddlers have not yet mastered the motor skills necessary for small hand movements.
2. They have limited group experience and few social skills, which means they are shy and do not share readily.
3. They have a great deal of energy which is best channeled into movements like running, jumping, and so on.
4. They react strongly to any changes in their routines.
5. They are at a crossroads between dependence and independence, needing their parents near them, while wanting to do things for themselves.

6. Abstract concepts such as sketchy illustrations do not attract their interest.
7. They like to touch things and learn by physical contact with objects.

This curious mixture of insecurity, independence, and limited skills requires careful planning and preparation. A toddler storytime includes more visual aids and more repetition in the story and throughout the program than do traditional preschool storytimes. It also involves parents as active participants to help toddlers focus their attention, concentrate, and feel secure. A variety of media must be used in the program to capture interest, encourage cooperation, and promote retention.

Preparation of Participants

Enlist the help of parents to prepare their children for storytime. Keep in mind that many of these parents may have little experience with storytimes themselves, and may feel that little can be done with children at this age. One way to prepare both adult and child for storytime is a letter briefly describing the program and emphasizing the cooperation between parent, child, and storyteller necessary to keep the program at a high level. This information lets parents know what to expect, what is expected of them, and that they will be participants and not observers. (*See* Fig. 1.)

Directions, clarification of program elements, and your expectations should be given throughout the first program of each session. Make it an integral part of the program. For example, as children line up to enter the storyspace, tell them what to expect: "You will find carpet squares laid out on the

Parent and child attend storytime

flood inside. Both you and mom will sit together on one carpet piece. You choose which one you will share with mom." Speak to the child; the parent will listen and follow your directions. This makes both feel at ease and encourages them to be better listeners.

Physical Location

It is important that toddler storytimes take place in an isolated area free from outside interruption. Ideally this means a separate room with a door that closes. However, a small area cordoned off in a large room can be satisfactory. For libraries with no separate meeting facility, the storytime program can be scheduled when the library is not open to the general public.

A small, well-defined storyspace is essential, since toddlers need clear boundaries in their worlds. If not self-enclosed, define the area by arranging chairs, book carts or tables around it. Keep it cozy and slightly larger than the seating space needed for the group. Provide designated places (carpet samples or small cushions). Arrange these in a semi-circular fashion facing the storyteller. (*See* Fig. 2.) This ensures that your audience will be able to see and hear you clearly.

Make a ceremony of entering the storyspace all together. This gives parents and children a clear signal that the program is about to begin. Do not let participants straggle into the storyspace before the program starts. Parents will begin to chat with each other, a situation that will remain a problem during the storytime, and toddlers will run and play in an area that you want to keep free of this kind of activity.

Provide another place for parents and toddlers to wait giving them the opportunity to greet each other, chat, or play. It is a good idea to have simple puzzles or toys available to keep little hands busy and to funnel away any excess energy at this time. Be certain there are enough so that each child has one of his or her own with which to play.

Storytime participants in semi-circle seating arrangement

Storytimes for 2-Year-Olds

(name)_____is scheduled for storytime on

(day)_____at (time)_____am/pm for 20-30 minutes.

It begins on (date)_____.

For many children this will be their first group experience. To make it a
happy one, we ask your cooperation and assistance in the following ways:

1. Please discuss storytime with your child before you come, explaining
that there will be stories, fingerplays, puppets, games and songs, and
that you will participate together. Young children need to know what is
expected of them.

2. Bring only the toddler who is registered. Older or younger children
should not be a part of this activity.

3. Attendance is important. Activities of one week are dependent on
those shared the week before. Please call if you cannot attend.

4. Once the storytime program is in progress, no one will be admitted to
the storyspace. Two-year-olds are easily distracted and latecomers
become the focus of attention. Please plan to arrive early.

5. There will be name tags for your child and for yourself. They will
help everyone become acquainted and feel at ease.

6. We will hold each program in the StoryRoom and will enter together
when it is time to begin. There will be carpet samples on the floor for
seating. Please choose a place to sit with your child on your lap or in
front of you.

7. If your child becomes very restless or uncooperative, please step
outside for a few seconds. This helps everyone to concentrate on the
story program.

8. Plan to check out books for your child to take the storytime experience home with you. Some books will be in the StoryRoom.

9. You will receive a handout each week that lists books, fingerplays,
songs, and rhymes used in the program, and ideas for activities for you
and your child to do at home.

Our main goal is for everyone to have a good time. With your help, we
can develop and nurture your toddler's love of books and the library.
The library staff will be happy to assist you either before or after
storytime with selection of books or other library services.

Fig. 1: Sample Letter

Fig. 2. Storyspace arrangement

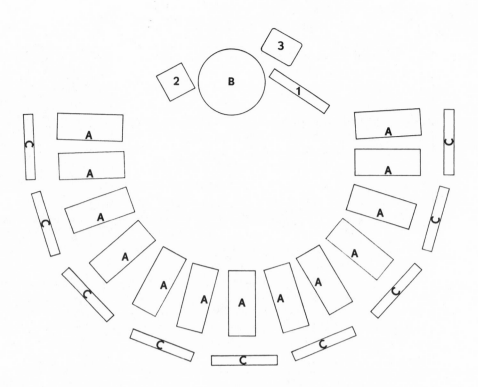

(A) Place carpet samples for seating toddlers and parents in a semi-circle so the storyteller is visible from each position.

(B) Storyteller sits on low stool or on floor with the following within an arm's reach: 1. Flannelboard on easel. 2. Low table or stool for display. 3. Storytime materials (books, puppets, flannelboard figures, handouts, and so on) in the order they will be used.

(C) Storyspace further defined by display books to be used in quiet time (and tables, book carts, or chairs as needed to define the area).

In the storyspace, display books providing a pleasant atmosphere for the program and making parents aware of other appropriate titles. These books can be exhibited on shelves, tables, or on the floor behind your audience. Use them to help define the storyspace.

Format

Each toddler storytime program should be 20–25 minutes in length with no more than ten toddlers and their parents at each session. The program is filled with fast-paced action and visual stiumuli divided into short (3–5 minute) segments. Four sessions of storytimes were offered each year, two in the fall and two in the spring; each session was six weeks long.

Time of day: It is little surprise that toddlers are more alert and cooperative in the morning than later in the day. Programs offered at 9:30am and 10:30am were both successful. Early evening programs (5:00 to 6:00pm) were also successful and provided an opportunity for working parents to attend with their children. We did not have good attendance or cooperation in the afternoons since most toddlers need to take naps.

The most important consideration is to select a time when there will be as few distractions as possible. Take the telephone off the hook if it can be heard in the storyspace. Take every precaution to keep from being interrupted. Once you have lost toddler attention, it is difficult to get it back.

Be consistent and firm about your program. If you decide that latecomers will not be admitted to a program in progress (and this is *strongly* recommended), make it clear from the beginning. Make no exceptions. It is unfair to those who have arrived on time to have their program interrupted by someone who is late. The opening routine prepares toddlers for the main part of the program, and if someone arrives late you have to begin again or contend with a very restless audience.

This may be an unpopular rule to parents caught in this situation. Latecomers are embarrassed and must deal with an angry, often tearful child when told they cannot join the group. If other staff members can run interference for you, have them explain the problems distractions cause and ask them to wait until the program is over so the child can get a handout and talk with a puppet. Staff members can offer an activity or toy to distract the child and give assistance in choosing books. Some parents will cooperate, and some will not. If they insist on entering the storyspace, don't cause a scene, but do talk to them about it after the program.

If a parent chooses not to stay, be certain to mail them a handout with a note stating that you are sorry they could not wait and how much you appreciate their cooperation in keeping the program of the highest level of quality. If you do not take your program seriously enough to enforce a rule about latecomers, neither will your audience. They will straggle in up to 20 minutes late! That is unfair to you, to other group members, and to the tardy child who has missed most of the program.

Toddler speaking to storyteller before program

Name Tags

Giving each child a name tag is an excellent way to greet them and a one-to-one experience for the storyteller and child. Name tags should be durable and laminated whenever possible to prevent little hands from pulling them apart. Attach them to the child's clothing with a safety pin or attach the tag to a piece of yarn placed over the child's head. Be certain that you are wearing a name tag that matches the child's. Providing one for each parent is a sign that they are to be participants and not observers.

Program Themes

Plan each program around a specific theme for easy selection of materials. A theme also helps toddlers focus and refocus their attention throughout the storytime as it is restated in the introduction of

each program element. Themes should be chosen carefully and should be objects or events familiar to toddlers: family members, daily routines, play activities, holidays, or animals. Support the theme with all other program elements: books, fingerplays, flannelboard stories, creative dramatics, music, and puppets.

Program Elements

Opening Routines

Opening and closing routines are the "security blankets" of storytime, helping toddlers to feel comfortable and safe. By keeping them exactly the same each week, you are giving clear signals to the children indicating where they are and what will happen next.

Create a ritual around entering the storyspace together. Use a sound-maker (a small whistle or a bell) to indicate that it is time to line up. March in together, reciting a nursery rhyme or singing a song. As each child chooses a place to sit, begin the storytime opening routine: an attention-getter, a fingerplay or song, and a flannelboard activity.

An attention-getter does just that! It is something that grabs the child's attention and focuses it on the storyteller. I prefer to gently touch each child. This stimulates one of the child's senses and rewards you with immediate response. A puff of air blown into their faces or tickling each child's ear gently with a feather says, "This will make you a good listener today."

Follow the attention-getter with a fingerplay. It keeps attention focused on you and provides a release for any restless energy. The fingerplay at this point shows both children and parents that they are expected to watch you, concentrate on what you are doing, and follow your lead.

After the fingerplay move immediately to a flannelboard activity. It is the basic introduction to the storytime concept for toddlers. For many this will be a first experience in watching and listening without being a direct participant in the activity. Here toddlers begin to learn listening skills and expand their ability to concentrate.

During this opening routine each child's attention progresses from self (a touch), to self and storyteller (participating in fingerplay), and finally to storyteller alone (flannelboard and storytelling). The child's thinking moves from the concrete to the abstract, a giant step for toddlers, reinforced and enhanced by storytelling.

Fingerplays

Fingerplays are very useful to toddler storytimes. Interspersed between stories they redirect restless energy and help toddlers refocus their attention on the storyteller. Fingerplays are excellent as an opening routine, a physical signal that it is time to settle down and listen. The combination of movement, rhythm and rhyme, plus the opportunity to follow directions, is a valuable addition to any storytime.

However, recall the last time you saw a toddler struggle to show his age on the fingers of one hand. Traditional fingerplays must be adapted for toddlers who have few motor skills. Create large, broad movements using the arms, legs, and body to replace the small finger-motions in your favorite fingerplays.

No child should be forced to participate in fingerplays or any activity during storytime. They will react strongly if pushed, rebelling and crying. It is not unusual for toddlers to sit and watch others during a fingerplay exercise. Encourage the parent to participate as a role model; the child will follow the parent's lead. Suggest that parents make time for fingerplay activities at home.

Incorporate sign language (American Sign Language or Signed English) into fingerplays whenever possible. Many signed words are appropriate for use with young children. It makes sense when teaching them a motion associated with a word to teach one that has meaning beyond the immediate situation.

Flannelboards

Small enough to hold in your hand or sitting on an easel and made from cardboard, wood or a carpet sample, a flannelboard is the backbone of a successful toddler storytime. With figures made from paper, felt, or fabric, it offers greater freedom and variety in programming than any other tool.

1. Flannelboard stories help hold the attention of toddlers because there is movement and action not only within the story but also in the telling of it. Toddlers like to watch the storyteller put figures on the flannelboard and take them off.

2. Since figures on a flannelboard can be touched and moved, another element that toddlers need is added to your program. A picture is an abstract concept. Toddlers cannot readily recognize and respond to the two-dimensional image in a picture as being representative of a "real" object. Although a flannelboard figure is also two-dimensional, it can be touched, held, and moved, forming a bridge between real and abstract.

3. Flannelboard figures allow the use of stories that may be too long or have illustrations inappropriate for use with toddlers in group situations. Always display the book from which the flannelboard story came. Although it may not be appropriate for group settings, many parents will want to check out that story to share with their toddler at home.

4. Flannelboards allow expansion of fingerplays, songs, and rhymes into visual formats, enhancing the storytime theme and providing additional material to fill a storytime program.

5. Flannelboard activites allow the use of elements which are unavailable in appropriate book form. We use a flannelboard figure of a

"Old MacDonald Had a Farm" flannelboard

stoplight during programs about colors and safety.

6. The flannelboard is a way that a story or rhyme can be repeated in different format, giving toddlers the repetition they need while keeping the material fresh for the storyteller and the adults in the audience.

Books

The selection of books for use in a toddler storytime is becoming easier as publishers respond to the need for toddler-oriented materials. There are many fine books available for this age. The criteria for choosing them follows.

1. The plot (if there is one) should be kept simple with no subplots.
2. The story should move quickly, from beginning to end, in a linear fashion with no flashbacks or references to events which did not happen in this story.
3. The subject of the book should be familiar to toddlers.
4. Characters should be kept to a minimum; no more than three or four.
5. Illustrations should be simple and clearly defined against their backgrounds, making it easy to focus on and identify the objects in the pictures.

6. Stories should be repetitive, either in the actions of the characters or in their dialogue.
7. The story should be adaptable for use in other media: fingerplays, flannelboards, creative dramatics, and puppetry.

Repetition is very important to young children, helping them to recall events and characters (memory and imagination), to anticipate action in the story (reading readiness), and listen to the words used in telling it (reinforcing vocabulary). Children greet a familiar story as an old friend and are eager to share it again and again. Therefore, the same story or rhyme used several times throughout the program is a good idea. Varying the format makes the repetition less tedious to the parents and the storyteller and stimulates the toddlers' senses.

Creative Dramatics

Creative dramatics come naturally to toddlers who love to play and pretend. It is an opportunity for them to stretch between stories, getting the "wiggles out" and preparing them to concentrate on what comes next. Keep it simple: ask the children to hop like a bunny, or fly like a butterfly, or chug like a train after stories with these themes.

Acting is also useful as an integral part in the telling of the story. When using *The Carrot Seed* by Ruth Krauss, toddlers may actively participate, pre-

Children "watering" seeds during Garden program

tending to plant the seed, water it, pull the weeds, and finally harvest a giant carrot from the storyteller's garden. They stay involved and follow the story from beginning to end.

Acting out elements in the story carries it beyond the moment of telling, helping toddlers recall what they have seen and heard. This develops a pattern for using their memories, filing, and retrieving information. It also enables them to re-examine, practice, and absorb some of the vocabulary used in the story. It encourages parents to play with their children and to see this "play" as the educational process that it is.

Music

Toddlers like to listen to music, dance and march to it, and sing. Music can be used when entering or leaving the storyspace as children line up to march with their parents. It can be coupled with storytelling, fingerplays, stretching activities, or creative dramatics.

Music can be made by the storyteller, by the entire group, and through use of phonographs or cassette tapes. Include as many different ways and opportunities as possible to incorporate music into the storytime program. Give the children the opportunity to play purchased or handmade instruments.

If you play an instrument, please incorporate it into at least one storytime. Children need to be introduced to music in all its varieties and sources. Always include singing a cappella so they can see

that music can be made without instruments. Do not say you cannot sing. *Everybody* can sing . . . some of us just don't carry tunes as well as others. Children do not care if you sing on key, and both parents and toddlers will recognize that it is your willingness to participate with them that is important.

Action songs with movements within them and those which have a lot of repetition are the best for toddlers. Words (instructions) should be sung clearly and actions kept simple and demonstrated by you. Songs with choruses or refrains such as *Old MacDonald Had a Farm* are popular.

Puppets

Puppets are one of the most popular parts of toddler storytimes for many reasons. They provide a nonthreatening introduction to the storyteller, to a new environment and routines, and to being in a group for the first time. They allow close physical contact between the child and the storyteller, important in building trust and friendship. Puppets add another tactile element to the program as each child can touch and be touched by them.

Puppets are usually smaller than toddlers who are used to being smaller than everyone else around them. This gives the children a feeling of importance and self-confidence. Talking and listening to a puppet is an opportunity for children to practice language skills, and this interaction helps children to recall the storytime program later at home.

Puppets should have specific jobs during storytime, such as:

1. a host, saying hello and goodbye, or leading participants into the storyspace and through opening or closing routines;
2. an assistant to the storyteller, introducing the theme of a story, giving directions for what comes next, and leading songs, fingerplays or creative dramatics activities throughout the program;
3. a role model, displaying both preferred behavior (sitting quietly and listening to the story) and undesirable behavior such as crossing the street without an adult (the children in the audience then participate by explaining the correct behavior);
4. a participant in telling the story, narrating or assuming the part of a character in it.

A puppet who says goodbye to children as they leave is essential. Toddlers need time to interact, to talk and hug and kiss; to absorb and react to the program and its elements; and to prepare themselves to leave the premises. Puppets are an excellent medium for this.

Puppets are inexpensive to buy and easy to make from material or objects found around the house. They should be sturdily constructed with no small pieces (eyes, noses, and so on) which can become detached and swallowed. They should be washable (felt cannot be washed). When making puppets, place the eyes relatively close to the mouth. This makes them less threatening. Avoid puppets with teeth for the same reason.

A host puppet should be made from soft fabric or fur and look inviting to touch or hug. The puppets used in the storytime are not toys, and children should not be allowed to play with them. Find some sturdy, washable puppets to include with the playthings available for children to use before and after storytime. Some easy-to-make puppets can be found in the Appendixes.

Quiet Time

A quiet time may seem out of place in a highly structured program whose emphasis is on action. However, it fits in well and serves several purposes.

1. Quiet time is an opportunity for parents to interact "one-to-one" with their children, in a supervised playtime; a few moments of sharing language (reciting rhymes or identifying body parts, colors, clothing, and so on); or choosing and looking at books together. This provides a model of interaction for both parent and child that encourages them to re-create it at home.
2. A few quiet moments allow the storytime experience to settle into the child's mind before the flurry of activity associated with leaving the library occurs. They will retain more of the program, re-create it and talk about it more at home when given this opportunity.
3. It is a good change of pace for toddlers. The storytime was filled with fast-paced, structured elements. This unstructured time lets them slow down and prepares them for closing routines and goodbyes.

Be aware that some parents may use this time to chat with each other rather than interact with their children. Give directions to the children to get parents involved: "Bobby, show mother this puzzle," or "Allie, take this book to your dad." Make it clear that this is part of the storytime program, not a visiting time and be firm about it. If they don't take the hint, discuss it with the parents after the program, pointing out that talking is distracting to others and that they can visit before or after storytime.

This quiet or "free" time will be short, as are all parts of the program. Usually after 2–5 minutes the children will become restless. At the first sign of restlessness in two or more children, begin the closing routine. It is a wonderful sight, however, when they are all so engrossed in the quiet activity with their parents that you must interrupt them to close the program.

Closing Routine

The closing routine should be the same each week: removing name tags, reversing the action of the attention-getter from the opening routine, handing out the program handout, saying goodbye to the puppet, and lining up to march out of the storyspace. Begin the closing routine by asking that name tags be removed and returned to you. This is a good way to refocus attention on you while allowing those still engrossed in the quiet activity to finish what they are doing.

Include a reversal of the attention-getter from the opening routine: if you use a feather to tickle the right ear at the beginning of the program, you can tickle the left ear during the closing routine.

A puppet should be used to say goodbye and to give each child an opportunity to talk, hug, or kiss it farewell. This physical contact during farewells (child, storyteller, and puppet) is reinforcing and reassuring to the child. Leave the storyspace with as much ceremony as you entered it, marching out to music or a chanted rhyme.

After the program don't hurry them out of the library. Let them look for books, chat, or play with toys. They may be reluctant to leave; remember that the next time you hear a teenager remark disparagingly about *having* to go to the library! However, if a parent is trying to get a stubborn child to leave, become involved by having the puppet wave goodbye and saying, "See you next week!", or direct the child's attention to something outside the library. The parent will be grateful for your assistance, and you won't have a screaming child leaving your premises.

Handouts

As part of the closing routine give each child a handout listing books, fingerplays, activities, and a craft. These informative handouts encourage parents and children to talk about storytime and do fingerplays and crafts together at home. The handouts assist parents with selection of books and make them aware of the importance of their role in their children's education. The handout keeps the library at their fingertips for many weeks to come. We often see parents months after a toddler storytime session has ended using these handouts to look for books.

The handout should include:

1. titles of stories used in the storytime program that day, including author's name and call number;
2. titles of other books and materials in your collection appropriate for toddlers and their location in the library;
3. words and directions for fingerplays, rhymes, and songs used in the storytime program;
4. one or two follow-up activities for the parent and child to do at home; and
5. a simple craft idea to be created at home. This is a good place to give instructions for making some of the materials and tools used in the storytime program (flannelboard, touchbox, sock puppet, and so on)

Distributing the handout at the end of the program provides you with another one-to-one contact with your storytime children. Give handouts to the toddlers with directions for them to pass them on to their parents. This provides an opportunity for them to follow directions, shows your con-

fidence in their abilities, and redirects any restless energy that might appear at the end of the program.

Handouts should be mailed to any absent child as a reminder that they were missed. Toddlers love to get mail, and parents soon depend on the handouts for the wealth of information in them. It also shows how seriously you take your program. This courtesy alone has earned this program high marks from parents.

Chapter 3 details a sample program and Chapter 4 provides 33 themes with handouts and notes about storytime program content.

Preregistration and Statistics

The nature of a toddler program with a limited number of participants demands preregistration. The size of the group must be limited to 10 or 11 children, and you will need both toddler and parent names well in advance of the first program to make name tags.

Preregistration also lets you determine whether or not another session is necessary to meet the demand in your community. By keeping a waiting list for those who want to register after the program is filled, you are provided with a mailing list for future programs.

When parents preregister their children for programs, they tend to take them more seriously and are less likely to be absent or tardy. By explaining that enrollment is being limited to provide the highest quality program possible for children, most parents will readily accept preregistration requirements.

Statistics (enrollment, attendance, number of programs, and so on) should be compiled for all library programming. Although time- and labor-intensive, programming is one area for which statistics and population-service information are usually unavailable. Therefore, it is the one often cut back in a budget crunch. Protect your investment by documenting it as thoroughly as possible.

3
Sample Program

The storytime program begins when the child enters the library and receives a name tag. This initial contact between storyteller and child will set the tone for the entire program series and cannot be underemphasized. The friendship and trust you create with the child at this point will translate into cooperation during your actual program. Ask your participants to arrive 10–15 minutes early so that they have ample time to settle down, get their name tags, and feel comfortable.

Greet the children from a low, stationary position; sitting in a chair near the entrance works well. Toddlers are usually shy in initial encounters and may feel threatened by unknown adults, especially when those adults are standing or moving toward them. It is also important for your face to be seen by the children. When you consider the perspective from which they view the world, you realize that everything looks huge to them and they see mostly kneecaps. Stay low, sit still, and let them come to you.

Everyone should wear name tags: the storyteller to set an example, the parent to act as a role model, and the child to give the storyteller a handle (the child's name) with which to control the program. The first close contact between the storyteller and the toddler is the name tag exchange.

After the parent and child have removed their wraps, ask them to come to you to receive their name tags. Be patient and resist the urge to go to them if the child is reluctant or slow. Letting them come to you reduces stress for the child and pro-

motes trust. To encourage the child to approach you, hold out the name tag and say, "Come see what I have for you." Children should not be forced to approach the storyteller for a name tag. If the child is still reluctant, get them involved in another way by asking them to "help" you distribute the parents' name tags. "Would you give this to your mommy, please?" Toddlers love to help. Continue to enlist their help in distributing name tags for parents each week.

Resist well-meaning parents' attempts to help you by taking their own name tags or offering to pin on their child's name tag for you. It is important that you come into close contact with the child to create a friendship bond.

Once you have the child close to you, show him his name tag and ask where the child would like to have it pinned. In cases of very shy children, let them watch as you pin a name tag on another child

Toddler receives name tag from storyteller

Children waiting in library
before program

for reassurance. Again coax them close by showing them their name tags, and comparing it to yours which matches it. This usually solves any reluctancy problems.

When you ask for cooperation or give instructions in this program, it is important that you speak to the children, not the adults. This fosters a bond of friendship. Tell the children what you want them to do; parents will comply if the child does not react. Also, do not rush when you talk to toddlers. They need time to assimilate what you are saying to them. Be patient with them and allow gaps of silence between requests, and repeat your request if necessary. If you begin to talk directly to the adults, you have indicated to the children that they are no longer important and their behavior will mirror that.

Before Entering Storyspace

Toddlers need time to become acclimated before a program begins. Being cooped up in a car or bundled in layers of clothing can make them very restless. Once their name tags are on, let them browse for books or play until it is time for the program to begin. Provide appropriate puzzles or toys with which they can play before the program begins. Toddlers do not share easily, so have enough for each child. Parents will soon learn that this pre-liminary time will be for them to chat or choose books, and that they are expected to participate fully in the storytime. This free time expells a lot of restless energy before you enter your storyspace.

Begin your program on time. It is a courtesy to those who have arrived on time, and it shows good discipline. If you do not take your own program seriously enough to begin on time, no one else will either. The result will be people arriving late, many disruptions during the program, and a less pleasant experience for everyone. In unusual weather or traffic conditions, ask those present before you delay beginning the program.

When it is time to begin, ask the children to gather their parents and line up to enter the story-space. Reassure children who are involved with a puzzle or toy that they can return to it after the storytime is over. By making the children responsible for getting their parents lined up, you are sending them another signal that you expect participation from them in the storytime program. It is important to enter the storyspace all together. Remember, you are in charge, and the more highly structured the routine is, the more secure toddlers feel and the greater their cooperation will be.

Within the storyspace you should have already placed seating markers to indicate where you want each parent and child to sit. Carpet samples are perfectly sized and economical as seating markers. Ask each child to find a place to sit.

Opening Routines

Attention-Getter: Expect a great deal of restlessness as everyone finds a place to sit and gets settled, but do not wait for them to settle down. Begin your program as soon as all have found places to sit. Start with something that grabs their attention and tells them that it is time to settle down, watch, and listen. This "attention-getter" should be something they can "feel": a puff of air or a soft object like a feather, puppet, or furry glove.

I discovered the need for an attention-getter during my first toddler storytime. I was surprised at all the commotion as they were settling down and realized that I needed something to focus their attention on me. I was carrying an empty basket which had contained name tags, and reaching into it, I ladled handfuls of air into my cupped hand, telling the children that it was "magic dust" to make them good listeners. I blew some magic dust toward each child. The puff of air immediately got their attention, and all of them watched carefully as each child received his gift of "dust." I since have used a paper fan to distribute the magic dust to each child (which has the effect of the puff of air while guarding against the spread of germs).

Once your storytime has begun, it must flow smoothly and continuously. Don't expect a lot of response from toddlers at first. You will need to proceed from one element in your program to the next without delays. Toddlers need a lot of structure. The pattern used in your program should not vary from week to week, but flow smoothly from opening to closing routines in the same order. The structured format may seem restrictive at first; however, you and your audience will feel more comfortable knowing what you are doing and when.

Fingerplay

Once you have the children's attention, proceed at once with the next element of the opening routine: a fingerplay. Choose one with easy-to-follow actions and sound-making (like hand clapping). I use this old standard:

Open Them, Close Them

Open them, close them, (open then close hands)
Open them, close them,
Give a little clap. (clap)

Open them, close them, (repeat)
Open them, close them,
Put them in your lap. (hands in lap)

Creep them, creep them, (hands move slowly up front of chest)
Up to your chin. (hands stop at chin)
Open your mouth, (mouth open)
But don't put them in. (hands behind back)

Open them, close them, (repeat actions above)
Open them, close them,
Give a little clap.
Open them, close them,
Open them, close them,
Put them in your lap.

Flannelboard

The flannelboard activity that I use is a shape puzzle. It is a group of seven basic shapes: two circles, a rectangle, a triangle, two stars, and a crescent. These shapes are displayed, named and then rearranged on the flannelboard to create a face of a clown, which matches the children's name tags. The children enjoy finding the same shapes in their own name tags. It does not take long before these toddlers are eagerly participating, calling out the names of the shapes as you rearrange them, identifying the completed figure, and making the connection to their name tags.

The three-step opening routine (attention-getter, fingerplay and flannelboard activity) gets them settled, relieves restlessness, and focuses their attention on you. When it is complete, introduce the theme for the program. This theme is reinforced

Flannelboard made from carpet sample

throughout the program and acts as a thread uniting all elements and activities.

Body of the Program

For purposes of demonstration I have chosen the theme of *Bears.* The following outline of program elements will be detailed using this sample theme; however, the elements can be adjusted as needed for other themes.

Stories

Two or three "stories" are the focal points of a storytime program and carry the program theme. They can be told with a picture book, displayed on a flannelboard, make use of a puppet, involve participation through creative dramatics, or any combination of these. For the first story choose the one that requires the most concentration in the program.

Begin the story immediately and focus your attention on the children who are listening to you, ignoring any child who has been distracted. By concentrating on those listening, you are not penalizing them for someone else's inattention. You are also giving the parent of the distracted child a signal that they need to refocus their child's attention. This makes clear to parents that they are responsible for disciplining their own children during the program.

Sample: In this example the first story will be *Sleepy Bear,* by Lydia Dabcovich. This colorful picture book

Storyteller holding book in proper position

is held up in front of the children and introduced by title. Continue to hold the book open toward the children as the story is told; the pages are turned so that they can see the illustrations as they listen to the story.

Slowly move the book from side to side as you tell the story. This added motion ensures that everyone can see and helps to keep all eyes focused on the illustrations.

Action Break

When the story is finished, be prepared with an action break. This gets the children up and moving: a fingerplay, a stretching exercise, or acting out some portion of the story. This movement allows toddlers to release their pent-up energy and helps them concentrate on what follows. If you do not provide them with a release, they will create their own. This pattern of concentration and release gradually lengthens their attention span and teaches toddlers how to concentrate. Be certain to use this opportunity to tell them how proud you are that they are being such good listeners.

Sample: Displaying the book *Sleepy Bear* on a low table, I ask everyone to stand, and I tell them I like to see bears. I immediately begin the fingerplay/rhyme:

Bears Everywhere

Bears, bears, bears everywhere (point around room)
Bears climbing stairs (making climbing motion with legs)
Bears sitting on chairs (pretend to sit)
Bears collecting fares (make a taking motion with hands)
Bears giving stares (eyes wide, peer around room)
Bears washing hairs (rub fingers briskly in hair)
Bears, bears, bears everywhere! (point again)

Take it slowly and overemphasize all the actions. If only a few children cooperated, repeat the rhyme, asking for everyone to help you (point out that parents will become involved too). Do not be concerned if a few children still prefer to watch. The important thing is that they stand up to release some energy before they sit down again.

Story-Action-Story

As soon as the children are seated after their action break, proceed with your next story in whatever form it may be, and follow it with another action break. This "story-action-story" pattern should continue in quick sequence throughout the program.

In the first few programs tell only two stories, interspersing them with longer action breaks. As attention spans lengthen and you become more familiar with your audience, you can tell more and longer stories with shorter action breaks. Be certain to leave enough time for a quiet time and a closing routine to end your program.

Sample: After we sit down from the action rhyme, I direct their attention to the flannelboard. I place ten felt bears on the board (counting them as I do), and hold up the book *Ten Bears in My Bed,* by Stan Mack. I then display the book on the storytelling table and proceed using only the flannelboard.

I ask them to show me ten fingers, holding my hands open wide in front of me. State that it would be hard to sleep with ten bears in your bed, and begin the song. (It can be chanted as a rhyme if you prefer.)

Ten Bears in My Bed

There were ten bears in his bed (hold up ten fingers)
And the little one said,
"Roll over! Roll over!" (roll hands over each other)
So they all rolled over (repeat hand rolls)
And one fell out. (remove one bear from flannelboard)
[Repeat with: Nine, eight, etc.
After the last bear: The little one said, "Good night!"]

If the group is older or has storytime experience, I have each child come forward and remove a bear during the rhyme. The bear is held and "rolled" until all are gone. Then the bears are returned to the flannelboard one at a time as we count them. The bears are removed from the flannelboard and placed out of sight as instructions are given for everyone to stand up for a stretching activity.

Use a stretching fingerplay or make it up as you go. As before with the previous activity, speak slowly and exaggerate your movements.

reach your hands up high, stretch . . . stretch . . .
   stretch;
now, reach down low and touch your toes;
stand up tall, arms open wide . . . lean right . . . lean
   left;
bring your arms in and give yourself a hug;
now, jump in place, first slow . . . then fast . . . now,
   slow again;
stand up tall, reach hands up high;
and now, sit . . . down . . . slow.

I introduce the next story which will be a participation story, and ask them to help me tell it. I tell them the story is about a bear hunt, and show them the actions to be used in it. We practice these together as I introduce them.

We are going on a bear hunt and will use our hands . . .
(pat them) on our knees to *walk* . . . and (pat faster)
run . . . *push* through tall grass . . . *swim* a river . . .
climb a tree . . . and *look* for a bear.
I'm ready to go. Who wants to go with me?
Get your hands ready (poised above knees) and
   let's go!

Go through the participation story as described on the handout for *Bears* found elsewhere in this book. At the end everyone is excited and needs to be calmed down. I introduce a bear puppet whose name is Benjamin, and he delivers "bear hugs" to the children and instructions for them to proceed into the quiet time activity.

Quiet Time

I feel strongly about bonding storytimes to hands-on experience with books. A quiet reading time has been included in the program for this purpose. Parents and children spend a few minutes looking at a book together and choosing one to take home with them.

Ask the children to choose a book to share with their parents. This gives them the power of selection and lets them see themselves as "helpers." They cooperate far better in this role than in any other.

Books were selected by the storyteller before the program and displayed around the storyspace behind the audience, either standing on the floor or on low shelves or tables. This allows the children to see them readily and choose one easily.

Additional copies of titles used in storytime are good for this purpose, but this is an excellent opportunity to display titles appropriate for sharing one-to-one and other books for toddlers whether or not they support the program theme. Always display a few more books than the number of participants in your storytime. Some will want to take more than one.

Give instructions for the children to "show the book" to their parents, then relax and watch a

Sock puppet "licks" finger of storytime participant

terrific sight: child and parent enthralled in books! The ability to concentrate on sharing a book one-to-one is also linked with a child's maturity. Some children may not have learned this skill; thus, programs early in the series will have short quiet times compared to later ones, where you have to interrupt this sharing just to finish the storytime.

Use quiet time to unobtrusively rearrange the storytelling area, putting things away and preparing for the closing rituals. This is easy to do while keeping an eye on the action in the room at the same time.

Closing Routines

Name Tag Removal

As the children finish looking at their books or become restless, tell them to have their parents remove both name tags. Then ask the children to bring the name tags to you. Trade each child a theme handout for the name tags. This becomes disorganized and noisy, and another attention-getter is needed to prepare the children for your closing routine.

Attention-Getter

I reverse the attention-getter used in the opening routine, and I ask the children to brush off the magic dust and to blow it back into my hands. This "dust" is then dumped back into my basket to produce the puppet (below).

Puppet

At some point earlier in the program (during quiet time) I secreted a sock puppet in the basket. When the magic dust is poured into the basket, the puppet appears . . . to the delight of the children and parents!

This puppet is "a finger-taster," and one by one he asks the children if he can "taste" a finger. If a finger is offered, the puppet gently "licks" it to see what "flavor" the child is that day. Select flavors familiar to toddlers: banana, bubble gum, french fry, milk, mashed potato, and so on.

Proceed slowly from child to child, never making sudden movements with the puppet and always respecting a child's desire not to participate. This reinforces trust in you and minimizes any negative feeling toward the puppet as an unknown object. Remember that the puppet is very real to them. Even though they watch you put it on your hand, it is perceived as a separate entity from you.

This puppet will become one of the most popular parts of your storytime program, and you will soon cherish the special contact between child and storyteller at this time. It is a terrific way to end each storytime program.

Goodbyes

After the puppet has "tasted" each child, announce that storytime is over for the day and thank everyone for being good listeners. Move with the puppet to the storyspace exit, asking the children to line up. When everyone is in line, march out of the storyspace as you entered it, singing or chanting together.

Outside the storyspace invite the children to come and say goodbye to the puppet before they leave with their parents. Sit in the same place where you greeted them as they came into the library, down low enough for the children to readily reach the puppet. Parents can gather up their belongings and books or get wraps ready while the children are engaged with the puppet and getting ready to leave.

Children use this opportunity to have their fingers "re-tasted" (you do not have to remember the flavor, the child will), to talk to the puppet, hug it, and kiss it goodbye again. If possible, each child should be allowed to say goodbye to the puppet and storyteller in his own way and take as long as he or she wants. When they depart, tell them, "See you next week!" This reinforces the on-going nature of your program and lessens any anxiety the child may feel about leaving.

For the last program in the storytime series a few changes in the closing routines need to be made. The children will keep their name tags instead of returning them to you at the end of the program. Tell them this at the end of quiet time and ask them to come up and get the handout. Be prepared for some children who insist you take the name tag during this exchange . . . they are creatures of habit. When that happens, give the name tag to the parent as you leave the storyspace.

I also tell them that they can take the magic dust home with them on the last day, but I have extra (in my pocket) to pour into the basket to make the puppet appear. And when saying goodbye, allow more time with the puppet for each child to say goodbye or to chat and remind them to come visit you often at the library.

If a child is absent during the last program, mail the handout and name tags. Be sure to note that it was the last program and invite parent and child to visit the library soon.

On the surface this program seems more rigidly structured than it is. The structure creates a framework on which many themes, activities, stories, local color, and individual talents are hung, making it more flexible than it initially appears and creating a toddler program unique to your needs and circumstances.

4
Suggested Programs

his chapter is a collection of ideas for thematic programs and handouts, in addition to program notes. The first part of each theme, *Babies,* for example, lists the stories used in the storytime program as well as additional books with similar themes appropriate for use with toddlers. Additional titles generally were not used in the storytime program either because their format made them inappropriate for use in a group situation or the storyteller preferred to use a different title.

Fingerplays, action rhymes, or songs used in the program are listed next, followed by ideas for parents and children to pursue together at home. A craft idea completes each theme.

The first part of each program constitutes a handout which, when copied, can be given to parents at the end of each storytime.

The program notes section is intended to assist storytellers with the actual mechanics of the program. Supplementing the information on the handouts, these notes offer ideas about sequencing, activities, and use of puppets for each program theme. This is included to ease some of the anxiety that beginning storytellers feel at the start of a new program: What comes first? Then what? How was that used?

These are *suggestions* only and intended to be guidelines to get a program started. Selection of stories and fingerplays, puppets, activities, and their place in the sequence of individual storytimes should be evaluated, manipulated, deleted or appended to create a program based on individual preferences, talents, and skills.

Although suggestions for many elements are given for each program theme, it is not necessary (or desirable) to include all of them in your weekly program. For example, I do not recommend providing a giveaway item each week. When used sparingly, giveaways do not become the prime focus of the storytime program.

The following key is used in program notes:

Before Program Instructions to be given the week before to parents

Opening Routine Attention-getter, fingerplay, and flannelboard shape puzzle are the basic routines. Add them to other suggestions given in this category in the sample programs.

Sign Sign language

ST Story (book; flannelboard; puppets)

A Action break

CD Creative dramatics

P	Puppet involvement
QT	Quiet time activity (looking at books together unless otherwise specified)
G	Giveaways (additional to the handout)
Closing Routine	Name tag removal, handouts, attention-getter, puppet farewell, exiting storyspace, and goodbyes are the basic routines. Many of the sample programs offer additional ideas in this category.
Notes	Personal notes, additional titles, fingerplays, and so on.

Instructions for construction of program materials frequently used in the storytime appear in the Appendixes.

Babies

Stories Shared

The Baby
JOHN BURNINGHAM

Peter's Chair
EZRA JACK KEATS

More Stories to Share at Home

Baby's Lap Book
KAY CHORAO

Zoo Babies
DONNA GROSVENOR

We Are Having a Baby
VIKI HOLLAND

*Hush Little Baby
A Folk Lullaby*

Knee Baby
MARY JARRELL

Big Brother
ROBERT KRAUS

I Am Adopted
SUSAN LAPSLEY

Sleep, Baby, Sleep
GERTRUDE OBERHANSLI

Animal Babies
TONY PALAZZO

Peggy's New Brother
ELEANOR SCHICK

On Mother's Lap
ANN HERBERT SCOTT

That New Baby
SARA STEIN

Betsy's Baby Brother
GUNILLA WOLDE

Rhythms, Rhymes, and Fingerplays

The Baby

Shhh! Be quiet! (finger to lips)
The baby is sleeping. (hands to cheek, palms together)
Shhh! Be quiet! (repeat motion each time)
The baby is sleeping. (repeat motion each time)
Shhh! Be quiet!

The baby is sleeping.
And we don't want to wake him up. (shake head slowly)

Walk on tiptoe, (touch fingers lightly on knees)
And don't make a sound. (finger to lips) . . . (repeat twice more)
'Cause we don't want to wake him up. (shake head slowly)

The baby woke up! (surprise motion: hands up by shoulders)
He's crying, boo-hoo. (fists to cheeks, rotate back and forth) . . .
(repeat twice more)
What are we going to do? (shake head slowly)

Let's tickle the baby, (wiggle fingers under chin)
Under the chin . . . (repeat twice more)
We want that baby to smile! (nod head briskly)

The baby stopped crying! (fists to cheeks, crying motion)
He's starting to smile! (display big smile) . . . (repeat twice more)
Now we are all happy again. (nod head slowly)

Follow-up Ideas

Toddlers should have soft toys to cuddle and play with regardless of their gender. They are never too young to learn to show tender, loving care for toys, pets, or other children.

What are they called? Animal babies are called by many different names. Expand your toddler's vocabulary by sharing these names in a game. Use a picture book or coloring book for animal pictures and say, "Here's a dog! Baby dogs are called puppies. What are they called? Puppies!"

cat—kitten	bird—chick	cow—calf
horse—colt	duck—duckling	bear/lion—cub
goat—kid	sheep—lamb	rabbit—bunny

Craft

Bubble Cup

You will need: small plastic/paper cup (5 oz. size)
old washcloth or piece of terry cloth
rubber band
plastic straw
hole punch
liquid soap
spray bottle with water in it

Punch a hole in the side of the cup one inch from the top. The straw should fit snugly in this hole. From the washcloth cut a circle larger than the mouth of the cup and secure it over the top of the cup with the rubber band. Spray water on the cloth to moisten it and smear a little liquid soap over it with your finger.

Have your child blow into the straw and bubbles will erupt from the top!

Since there is only air inside the cup, the child will not get soap or water in the mouth if he or she sucks on the straw instead of blowing. If the bubbles stop, check to see if the straw is bent, cutting off the air supply. Also, check the cloth to determine if more water or soap is needed.

Cups can be labeled with the child's name and decorated with markers, fabric scraps, or pictures. The cloth can be removed and washed or replaced as needed.

Program Notes

Before Program	Invite children to bring a favorite toy or doll.
Opening Routine	Introduce the storytime with a baby doll or puppet, giving each child the opportunity to cradle, rock, or tuck the baby into a shoe box or basket bed. Emphasize that toddlers are "big boys and girls" and different from babies.
Sign	"Baby"—Form a cradle with arms as if holding a baby. Gently rock arms from side to side.
ST	Book: *Peter's Chair*
A	"The Baby" fingerplay
ST	Display book: *The Baby*. Tell story using flannelboard figures.
P	Puppet is dressed as a baby and displays baby behavior: crying, laughing, yawning, and so on.
CD	Taking care of baby. Each child rocks, cuddles, tickles their toy or doll ("baby") to mimic the storyteller's actions with the puppet.
QT	Child shares a book with parent and "baby."
G	I'm a Big Boy/Girl medals
	Needed: 3″ posterboard circle; 24″ ribbon or yarn
	Trace around water glass for circle pattern. Print message on circles, one for each child. Staple both ends of ribbon or yarn to top of circle to be slipped over child's head.
Closing Routine	Bring out puppet "baby" to say goodbye.

―――――――― **Notes** ――――――――

Bears

Stories Shared

Sleepy Bear
LYDIA DABCOVICH

Ten Bears in My Bed
STANLEY MACK

More Stories to Share at Home

Snow on Bear's Nose
JENNIFER BARTOLI

He Bear, She Bear
STAN BERENSTAIN AND
JAN BERENSTAIN

B Is for Bear
DICK BRUNA

Corduroy
DON FREEMAN

Do Baby Bears Sit in Chairs?
ETHEL KESSLER AND
LEONARD KESSLER

Milton the Early Riser
ROBERT KRAUS

Blueberries for Sal
ROBERT MCCLOSKEY

The Real Mother Goose
MOTHER GOOSE

I'm Going on a Bear Hunt
SANDRA SIVULICH

The Three Bears

Lazy Bear
BRIAN WILDSMITH

Rhythms, Rhymes, and Fingerplays

Bears Everywhere

Bears, bears, bears everywhere (point with index finger)
Bears climbing stairs (make climbing motion)
Bears sitting on chairs (sitting motion)
Bears collecting fares (pretend to accept change)
Bears giving stares (eyes wide open, look around)
Bears washing hairs (rub fingers in hair)
Bears, bears, bears everywhere! (point)

Going on a Bear Hunt

We are going hunting for a bear.
(shade eyes with hand and peer around)
We will walk down the sidewalk;
(pat hands on knees for walking)
Push our way through tall grass;
(alternately push hands away from body side to side)
Swim a river;
(make swimming motions)

And climb a tall tree.
("climb" as if pulling self up a rope, hands alternating)
Keep looking!!
(shade eyes and peer all around)
What do you see?? A Bear????
(act surprised)
We have to get out of here!
(repeat above motions faster)

Climb down that tree, and Run!
Swim that river, and Run!
Push through that grass, and Run!
Now Run up the sidewalk ... and in the door ...
And shut the door tight!
(Clap hands loudly)
Whew ... I'm glad we are home safe!!
(wipe forehead with fingers and sigh)

Follow-up Ideas

Guess what I am? This guessing game uses the sounds and motions of different animals. Toddlers like to guess, and they like to act out the different animals with you. Start with a picture book about farm animals to give you ideas and to reinforce the actions with a picture. These are also more familiar to your child.

Watch for bears when shopping or when travelling anywhere, look at magazines and books. This activity is fun since bear logos are plentiful. It helps your toddler become more observant.

Craft

Kitchen Clay

You will need: 2 cups baking soda
1 cup cornstarch
1⅓ cups water
pinch of salt

This recipe feels almost like *real* clay. Put all the ingredients in a saucepan and mix well. Stir over medium heat until the mixture bubbles and thickens. Turn out onto a board or waxed paper and let cool. Knead until smooth. Wrap in a damp towel and place in the refrigerator for 10–15 minutes. Help your child learn how to squeeze, roll, pat, and make balls from clay and to put them together to make many different objects.

Store the clay in a tightly closed plastic bag in the refrigerator, and add a few drops of water to the bag to keep it from hardening. To preserve a special creation, let the object harden in the air for a day or two. Paint with tempera or acrylic paints and cover with shellac. The result: a work of art!

Program Notes

**Opening
Routine**

Sign   "Bear"—Cross arms over the chest with hands on shoulders. Scratch twice on shoulders.

ST   Book: *Sleepy Bear*

A   "Bears Everywhere" fingerplay

ST   Display book: *Ten Bears in My Bed*. Flannelboard story: Remove ten felt bears on the flannelboard one at a time as you chant or sing the song. Each child can return one of the bears to the flannelboard at the end of the song (or in cooperative groups, let each one take a bear from the flannelboard during the song).

A   Stretching

ST   "Going on a Bear Hunt" action story

P   A bear puppet is "discovered" at the end of the bear hunt. The puppet hugs and is hugged and gives out instructions for quiet time.

QT   Child and parent look at books together.

G   Bear straw caddy

Needed: Pattern enlarged to 4″ hole punch; plastic straw

Copy the pattern and cut out. Punch holes where indicated in top and bottom of bear. Thread straw through. Tape over straw on back if bear slides.

**Closing
Routine**   Bear puppet leads exit from storyspace and says goodbye.

---- Notes ----

Bedtime

Stories Shared

Ten, Nine, Eight
MOLLY BANG

Goodnight Moon
MARGARET WISE BROWN

Napping House
AUDREY WOOD

More Stories to Share at Home

Sleepy Little Lion
MARGARET WISE BROWN

Good Night
ELIZABETH COATSWORTH

Bedtime Story
J. M. ERSKINE

Baby Owl
YASUKO FUNAZAKI

Which Is the Best Place?
MIRRA GINSBURG

Goodnight Owl
PAT HUTCHINS

All the Pretty Horses
SUSAN JEFFERS

May We Sleep Here Tonight?
TAN KOIDE

Milton the Early Riser
ROBERT KRAUS

The Bundle Book
RUTH KRAUSS

Mother Goose Treasury

Peace at Last
JILL MURPHY

Goodnight, Goodnight
EVE RICE

Ira Sleeps Over
BERNARD WABER

Rhythms, Rhymes, and Fingerplays

Going to Bed

This little child is going to bed.
(point to self)
Down on the pillow he lays his head.
(rest head on hands)
He wraps himself in covers tight,
(wrap hands across body)
And this is the way he sleeps all night.
(close eyes, nod head)

Morning comes, he opens his eyes.
(raise head, eyes wide open)
Off with a toss the covers fly.
(fling arms wide)
Soon he is up and dressed and away,
(jump up)
Ready for fun and play all day.
(clap hands, turn in circle)

Rock-a-Bye-Baby

Rock-a-bye baby on a tree top,
When the wind blows the cradle will rock,
When the bough breaks the cradle will fall,
And down will come cradle, baby and all.

Follow-up Ideas

Look out the window just before bedtime to see if the rest of the world is going to sleep. What color is the sky at night? Is there a moon? What shape is it? Can you see lights? Are they moving, blinking, or standing still?

Bedtime is easier with a set routine. Sharing a book is a perfect way to help your child settle down and get ready for sleep.

Craft

Bedtime Mobile

You will need: branch with several smaller twigs

string (several pieces 12" long)

scissors

index cards

glue

pictures from magazines, photos, tin-foil shapes, small toys, or items from nature.

Cut out pictures, photos, or shapes and glue to both sides of an index card. Trim around the edges, and punch a small hole in the top of the card. Push one end of a piece of string through the hole and tie it in a knot. Tie the other end of the string to the branch and keep adding pictures, varying the length of the string and placement on the twigs. Hold the branch up often to see how it balances when hanging.

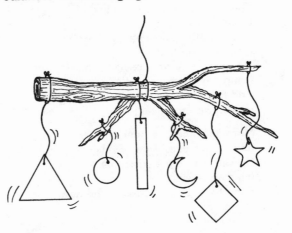

Find the center of the branch, and tie a string there. Attach the mobile to the ceiling over your toddler's bed with a nail or plant hanger. It will move in the air currents, helping little ones fall asleep as they watch it. Change the items on the mobile or make a new one as seasons change or holidays approach. Use small objects (toys, pine cones, leaves, and so on) light enough to balance each other. Let your child help you accumulate the items to be added to a new mobile and decide where they will be placed.

Program Notes

Before Program Invite children to attend in pajamas, slippers, and robes.

Opening Routine

Sign "Sleep"—With palms together, place hands next to your cheek and lean head against them (like a pillow).

ST Book: *Goodnight Moon*

CD In pantomime, prepare for bed and wake up in the morning (change clothes, brush teeth, yawn, and so on)

ST Display book: *The Napping House* (flannelboard story)

A "Going to Bed" fingerplay

ST Book: *Ten, Nine, Eight*

P Puppet gets ready for bed and gives each child a goodnight hug or kiss. Let each child tuck the puppet into bed for a nap during the quiet time. Place "I'm Sleeping" sign on puppet's bed.

QT Child looks at books with parent.

G Awake/Asleep doorknob hanger

Needed: Index cards; 18″ yarn; hole punch; marker

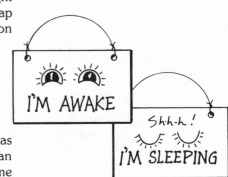

Decorate both sides of card with waking/sleeping eyes as shown. Punch holes in top corners and tie yarn in them. Can be hung on the child's door to be flipped over at naptime or bedtime.

Closing Routine Puppet wakes up to lead children from room.

─── **Notes** ───

Birthdays

Stories Shared

Spot's Birthday Party
ERIC HILL

Happy Birthday, Sam
PAT HUTCHINS

More Stories to Share at Home

The Secret Birthday Message
ERIC CARLE

Birthday Wish
ED EMBERLEY

Birthday Presents
EUGENE FERN

Ask Mr. Bear
MARJORIE FLACK

Mop Top
DON FREEMAN

Letter to Amy
EZRA JACK KEATS

Surprise for Danny
LOIS LENSKI

The Birthday Present
BRUNO MUNARI

The Birthday Party
HELEN OXENBURY

Surprise Party
ANNABELLE PRAGER

Benny Bakes a Cake
EVE RICE

Happy Birthday to Me
ANNE ROCKWELL

The Surprise
GEORGE SHANNON

Tall Book of Mother Goose

Rhythms, Rhymes, and Fingerplays

A Birthday

Today is (insert child's name) birthday
Let's make a birthday cake (form circle with fingers)
Mix and stir (make stirring motions)
Stir and mix,
Then into the oven to bake. (palm up, make sliding motion)

Peeking through the window (shade eyes with hands)
I like to see it bake.
Sniff, sniff, sniff. It smells so good! (sniff)
Hurry, hurry, cake! (clap hands sharply)

Here's our cake so nice and round (form circle with fingers)
We'll frost it pink and white. (make frosting motions)
We'll put two candles on it (hold up two fingers)
To make a birthday light.
And then, blow them out!! 1, 2. (blow on fingers)

Balloon

This is the way we blow our balloon
(hold hands, palms together, in front of mouth)
Blow!! Blow!! Blow!!
(blow into hands, pulling them apart slowly)
This is the way we break our balloon
(hands wide apart)
Oh!! Oh!! Oh!!
(clap hands 3 times)

Follow-up Ideas

Have a pretend birthday party (great for bad weather days). Invite dolls and stuffed animals and wrap up one of your child's old toys in paper; let your child help you do this. Devise a pretend birthday cake (a piece of bread, muffin, cookie) and sing "Happy Birthday" to the lucky person (or animal). Everybody helps blow out the pretend candles. This party can be given in honor of a friend, a favorite stuffed animal, or your child.

Toddlers like to pretend. Sometimes this pretense can help prepare them for new situations: parties, Sunday school, sharing with others. When confronted with an new situation, try acting it out at home ahead of time.

Craft

Birthday Clown

You will need: scissors

colored paper

3 rubber bands (cut in half to make 6 pieces)

tape

glue

2 paste-on stars

From the colored paper, cut these shapes:

2 large hearts (body)

2 small hearts (hands)

1 large circle (head)

3 small circles (pom-poms)

1 small crescent (mouth)

2 small rectangles (shoes)

Using these shapes, assemble the head, hat, pants and pom-poms to match the figure as shown. Glue a piece of rubber band to each shoe and hand, and then glue the other end to the back of the pants and shirt as shown. Attach another rubber band to the top of the hat.

When you dangle the clown, he will dance for you! To make the clown more durable, reinforce each shape with light cardboard (3″ × 5″ card) before assembling.

Program Notes

Opening Routine	Introduce the theme by singing "Happy Birthday" to a puppet who is wearing a party hat. The puppet invites children to join in his birthday celebration and promises a surprise later.
Sign	"Birthday"—Right hand open on chest. Move right hand out and down to lay, palm up, in open left hand.
ST	Book: *Happy Birthday, Sam*
A	"A Birthday" fingerplay
ST	Use a flannelboard birthday cake with candles that can be added or deleted. Let children take turns putting candles on cake, blowing them out, and taking them down.
A	Stretching
ST	Book: *Spot's Birthday Party*
A	"Balloon" fingerplay
QT	Child and parent look at books together.
G	Balloons, inflated and tied with string, are stored in the touchbox. Puppet, still wearing a party hat, invites children to feel inside and guess the surprise. He reminds them just to touch and not to pull anything out through the hole. The puppet then distributes balloons.
Closing Routine	Exit singing "Happy Birthday"; puppet gives birthday hugs during goodbyes.

Notes

Boats

Stories Shared

Mr. Gumpy's Outing
JOHN BURNINGHAM

Boat Book
GAIL GIBBONS

More Stories to Share at Home

Who Sank the Boat?
PAMELA ALLEN

Boats on the River
MARJORIE FLACK

The Little Sailboat
LOIS LENSKI

Hurrah, We're Outward Bound
MOTHER GOOSE

Noah's Ark

Henry the Castaway
MARK TAYLOR

If I Sailed a Boat
MIRIAM YOUNG

Rhythms, Rhymes, and Fingerplays

Meet the Boats

Toot, toot, toot,
(pretend to blow whistle)
chug, chug, chug,
I am a Tug . . . boat.
(arms push and pull in piston motion)
Row, row, row, to and fro,
(make rowing motion)
I am a Row . . . boat.
Wind puffs, blows a gale,
(blow into cupped hands)
I am a Sail . . . boat.
Drive fast; wheee, wheee,
(pretend to steer)
I am a Speed . . . boat.
Back and forth, people I carry,
(hands move across front of body and back)
I am a Ferry . . . boat.
Under water, blub, blub, blub,
(hands over head like surface of water)
I am a Sub . . . marine.

Row, Row, Row Your Boat

Row, row, row your boat
Gently down the stream.
Merrily, merrily, merrily, merrily,
Life is but a dream.

Follow-up Ideas

Sit on the floor facing your toddler and holding hands. Rock backward gently pulling your child toward you. Then have him rock backward as you lean forward. Sing the song "Row, Row, Row Your Boat" while you rock back and forth in a rowing motion.

In the sink, bathtub, or pool, try floating different objects to see which would make good boats. Styrofoam meat trays float well and "carry cargo," too.

Craft

Bathtub Boats

You will need: bottle cap or jar lid, bar of floating soap, cork, or empty walnut shell

toothpicks

dab of clay or clay dough

scissors

crayons

paper

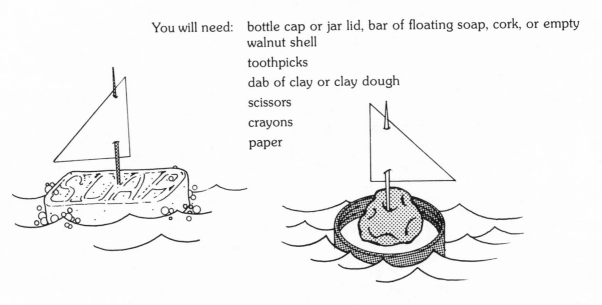

Cut a sail from the paper (triangle shape) and decorate it. Put your child's name on it. Poke a toothpick through the sail, through one side and out. Leave one end of the toothpick sticking down below the sail to anchor it to the boat. Stick a dab of clay inside the jar lid or shell, and press the toothpick into it. Your boat is now ready to sail.

If using cork or soap, the clay is not needed. Press the toothpick mast into the boat and set sail. If using a cork, cut a slit in one side and push a penny into it for balance.

Program Notes

Opening Routine Introduce theme with a puppet who has a toy or paper boat.

Sign "Boat"—Cup hands at waist level. Raise and lower slightly as you move them outward from your body (like a boat on waves).

ST Display book: *Mr. Gumpy's Outing* (flannelboard story)

A "Row, Row, Row Your Boat" (make rowing motions)

ST Book: *Boat Book*

A "Meet the Boats" fingerplay

CD Pass out boat stick puppets and have the children act out the motions a boat might go through: blowing in the wind, gliding fast, bobbing up and down on the ocean, diving under the sea, and so on. Have children "park" their boats in the boat garage (touchbox) after you finish.

QT Participants look at books together.

G Make paper boats from newsprint or typing paper. Let the children watch you fold one, then have a puppet distribute those you have made ahead of time.

Closing Routine All exit with boats held high, floating over heads.

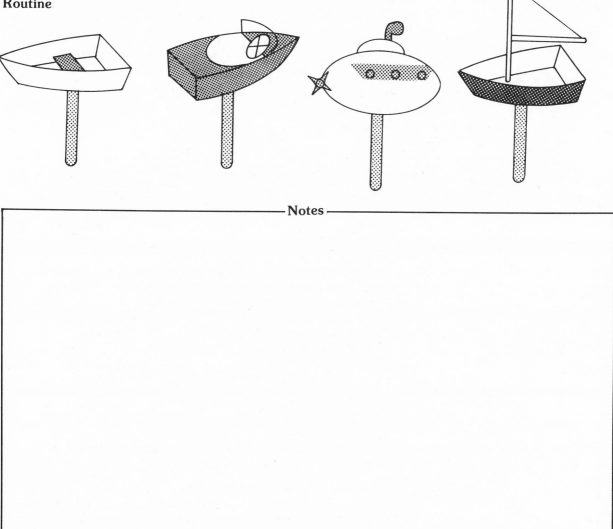

Notes

Bugs and Caterpillars

Stories Shared

The Very Hungry Caterpillar
ERIC CARLE

Inch by Inch
LEO LIONNI

Other Books of Interest

Buzz! Buzz! Buzz!
BYRON BARTON

Grouchy Ladybug
ERIC CARLE

One Dragon to Another
NED DELANEY

Never Say Ugh to a Bug
NORMA FARBER

Be Nice to Spiders
MARGARET B. GRAHAM

Changes, Changes
PAT HUTCHINS

The Caterpillar and the Polliwog
JACK KENT

Ladybird Quickly
JULIET KEPES

Zoo in My Garden
CHIYOKO NAKATANI

Blue Bug Goes to the Library
VIRGINIA POULET

*Ladybug, Ladybug and
Other Nursery Rhymes*
ELOISE B. WILKIN

Rhythms, Rhymes, and Fingerplays

Eency Weency Spider

Eency-weency spider went up the water spout,
(wiggle fingers upward in front of body)
Down came the rain and washed the spider out.
(sweep arms down and to one side)
Out came the sun and dried up all the rain,
(arms form circle over head)
And the eency-weency spider went up the spout again.
(wiggle fingers upward again)

Caterpillar

This is the egg, found not far away.
(point with index finger to center of other palm)
This is the caterpillar, who one sunny day
hatched from the egg, found not far away.
(wiggle index finger like caterpillar)

This is the cocoon all snuggled away
that covered the caterpillar, who one sunny day,
hatched from the egg, found not far away.
(form fist, cup other hand over it, peek inside)

This is the butterfly, who did sashay
out of the cocoon all snuggled away,
that covered the caterpillar, who one sunny day,
hatched from the egg, found not far away.
(slowly pull fist out of cupped hand and open fingers)

These are the wings, on bright display
worn by the butterfly, who did sashay
out of the cocoon all snuggled away
that covered the caterpillar, who one sunny day,
hatched from the egg, found not far away.
(palms toward you, hook thumbs together and wiggle fingers)

Beautiful butterfly . . . Can I watch you play?
("fly" your butterfly up, down, and around)

Follow-up Ideas

Make a nesting game with different sizes of cans. Cut one end cleanly open so there are no sharp edges. Cover the edges with adhesive or cloth tape. Cans may then be stacked upside down on top of each other to build things or nested inside each other for storage.

To make a finger puppet quickly and easily, cut the finger off an old glove. Decorate with markers, material, and yarn scraps or buttons to make eyes, ears, mouths, hair, and tails. Add felt wings to create a butterfly.

Craft

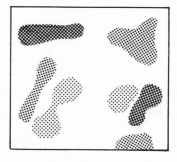

Colorful Butterfly

You will need: paper towels

newspapers

food coloring or tempera paint

sponge or small paint brush

pipe cleaners

small containers (baby food jars, margarine containers, muffin pan)

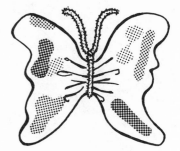

Cover the table with newspapers, several layers thick. Lay a paper towel flat on the newspapers. Pour food colors into separate containers for each color. With the sponge or paintbrush, help your child dab or drop each color onto the paper towel. See how the colors spread through the towel. Where they mingle, new colors are created. Clear water can be sprinkled on the towel to lighten or spread the colors more. Hang the towel and let dry thoroughly.

When dry, fold towel lengthwise in accordian pleats. Pinch together at the center of the towel and twist a pipe cleaner around it to hold. Curve the ends of the pipe cleaner to look like antennae, and fluff out the paper towel on both sides of the pipe cleaner to form wings. Decorate your windows or room with beautiful butterflies.

Program Notes

**Opening
Routine**

ST Book: *Inch by Inch*. Use a finger puppet as the inchworm and "inch" it through the book while telling the story, for example, measure the flamingo's neck, and so on.

A Stretch. Let inchworm measure arms, legs, feet, and hands.

ST Book: *Very Hungry Caterpillar*. Tell the story once using the book, then repeat briefly using the caterpillar sock puppet.

Sign "Butterfly"—Cross hands at wrists, palms facing chest. Link thumbs. Wiggle fingers together like butterfly wings.

A "Caterpillar" fingerplay

ST "Eency Weency Spider" stick puppets story using lap stage

A "Eency Weency Spider" action rhyme

QT Child and parent look at books together.

G Facial tissue butterflies

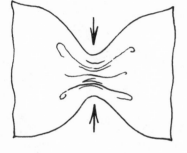

Needed: Colored or patterned facial tissues; pipe cleaners; pencil

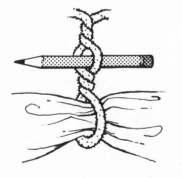

Gather the tissue together at the middle, creating two wings. Wrap center of pipe cleaner around the gathered tissue and twist twice. Insert pencil between pipe cleaner ends and twist again. Remove pencil (leaving the head made). Curl pipe cleaner ends into antenna and fluff out wings.
Puppet helps distribute butterflies.

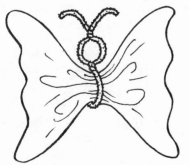

**Closing
Routine** Fly butterflies out of storyspace.

Notes

Chickens

Stories Shared

Rosie's Walk
PAT HUTCHINS

The Egg Book
JACK KENT

The Chicken Book
GARTH WILLIAMS

Other Stories of Interest

What Does the Rooster Say, Yoshio?
EDITH BATTLES

Little Chicken
MARGARET WISE BROWN

Rooster Who Set Out to See the World
ERIC CARLE

Chicken Licken

Good Morning, Chick
KORNEY CHUKOVSKY

Cock-A-Doddle-Do
BERTA HADER AND ELMER HADER

Little Chick's Story
MARY D. KWITZ

Little Red Hen and The Grain of Wheat

The Rooster Crows
MAUD PETERSHAM AND
MISKA PETERSHAM

Rhythms, Rhymes, and Fingerplays

Hen and the Chicks

Good Mother Hen sits on her nest,
(one fist in other cupped palm)
Keeps the eggs warm 'neath her soft breast,
Waiting, waiting, day after day.
(lift fist and peer into cupped palm)
Hark! there's a sound she knows very well,
(hand to ear)
Some little chickens are breaking the shell,
Pecking, pecking, pecking away.
(make pecking motion with pointer finger into palm of hand)
Now they're all out, oh, see what a crowd!
(wiggle fingers of one hand)
Good Mother Hen is happy and proud,
Cluck-cluck, cluck-cluck, clucking away.
(hands in armpits, flap elbows like wings)
Into the coop the mother must go,
(one hand behind back)
But all the chickies run to and fro,
(wiggle fingers of other hand back and forth in front of body)

Peep-peep, peep-peep, peeping away.
Here is some corn in my little dish,
(cup one palm upward)
Eat, Mother Hen, eat all that you wish,
Pecking, pecking, pecking away.
(repeat pecking motion)
Happy we'll be to see you again,
Dear little chicks and good Mother Hen!
(hold up fist and wiggle fingers of other hand)
Now good-bye, good-bye for today.
(wave goodbye)

Follow-up Ideas

Cut holes of varying sizes in a box. Using plastic eggs of different sizes, let your child drop them into the box. This is a good exercise for learning sizes. Hint: To store small plastic eggs from Easter, keep them in an egg carton.

Tossing or dropping bean bags into containers is good coordination activity. Bean bags can be dropped from above while standing or tossed toward containers. They are easily stored inside a coffee can or shoe box.

Craft

Bean Bag Chickens

You will need: old mittens or hot mitts
buttons for eyes
fabric scraps or felt for wings and beaks
glue
needle and thread
dried beans or rice

Hold the mitten up in front of you; the thumb will become the tail of the chicken and the opposite side is the chicken's head. Sew a button on each side for eyes and glue on a fabric triangle for a beak. Cut two semi-circles of material for wings and glue to each side of the body.

Fill the mitten loosely with dried beans or rice and sew the opening securely so that the beans will not fall out if roughly handled. Use scraps or yarn to create other animals or people out of other mitts.

Program Notes

Opening Routine Puppet introduces theme with a plastic egg with a small pom-pom chick hiding inside. The storyteller opens the egg to let the chick emerge, and it nestles somewhere to listen to the stories.

Sign "Chicken" (bird)—Pinch index finger and thumb of right hand together. Place it in front of your mouth like a beak, and open and close it.

ST Book: *Rosie's Walk.* Make clucking sounds throughout the book as Rosie progresses on her walk.

A Reenact Rosie's walk in the storyspace, walking around, through, and under, using the parents as objects in the story.

ST Display book: *The Chicken Book* (flannelboard story)

A "Hen and the Chicks" fingerplay

P   Puppet brings out a basket of plastic eggs, and gives one to each child to open. Inside are pom-pom chicks. Children then return eggs and baby chicks to the basket. (If you do not use them as giveaways, let the children say goodbye to them during closing.)

QT   Children and parents look at books together.

G   Pom-pom chicks

Needed: Yellow pom-poms; craft eyes; glue; felt scraps

Glue eyes, beaks, and combs on one pom-pom. Attach to second pom-pom and add feet. Have puppet distribute.

**Closing
Routine**

red

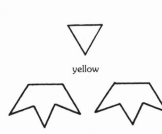
yellow

Notes

Clothing

Stories Shared

Charlie Needs a Cloak
TOMIE dePAOLA

How Do I Put It On?
SHIGEO WATANABE

More Stories to Share at Home

The Wonderful Shrinking Shirt
LEONE C. ANDERSON

Pelle's New Suit
ELSA BESKOW

Pocket for Corduroy
DON FREEMAN

Sara and the Door
VIRGINIA JENSEN

New Blue Shoes
EVE RICE

No Roses for Harry
GENE ZION

Animals Should Definitely Not Wear Clothing
JUDI BARRETT

I Can Dress Myself
DICK BRUNA

I Like Old Clothes
MARY ANN HOBERMAN

The Mother Goose Book

Max's New Suit
ROSEMARY WELLS

Rhythms, Rhymes, and Fingerplays

My Zipper Suit

My zipper suit is bunny brown
(point to chest)
The top zips up
(draw fingers upward from tummy to chest)
The legs zip down.
(draw fingers down leg)
I wear it every day.
(point to self and nod)
My daddy brought it out from town.
Hi, Daddy! (wave)
Zip it up, zip it down
(repeat above motions)
And hurry out to play.
(run in place)

Look at Me!

Look at me! (point to self)
Upon my head I wear a hat of brightest red. (hands on head)
Look at me! (point to self)
Don't I look neat with shiny shoes upon my feet? (point to feet)

Look at me! (point to self)
Hip hip hooray! (clap hands)
With shirt and pants (point to clothing)
I'm dressed to play. (jump up and down)

Follow-up Ideas

Set aside definite places for things in the home. Place clothes hooks or hangers low enough so your child can hang up his or her own clothes.

A good way to avoid right and left shoe mix-ups is to use a waterproof marker or laundry pen. Draw a dot on the inside of each shoe along the inner edge. With shoes sitting next to each other (correctly), dots will line up side by side.

Craft

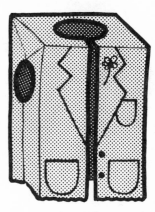

Paper Bag Costume

You will need: grocery sack

crayons or markers

paper or cloth scraps

glue

scissors

With the sack upside down, cut three holes in it: one on top for the head and one on each side for the arms. Cut in a line from the neck hole down the front of the sack to make it easier to get on and off.

Decorate sack with crayons, markers, or scraps. Add buttons, pockets, collar, belt, sash, or fringe. The costume can look like everyday clothes or be exotic: superheroes, wild creatures, and so on. Hang these costumes from hangers in an area where your child has access to them for fun and pretend play. Don't be surprised if older brothers or sisters want to be part of this, too.

Program Notes

Opening Routine Point out different kinds of clothing worn by parents and children to introduce theme.

ST Book: *Charlie Needs a Cloak.* Puppet, wearing a ragged cloth around his shoulders introduces the word "cloak," brings the book to the storyteller.

A "Look At Me!" fingerplay

Sign "Shirt"—Pinch shirt or blouse at shoulders and pull gently.

ST Display book: *How Do I Put It On?* Tell as flannelboard story.

A "My Zipper Suit" action rhyme

P Puppet appears carrying hat, scarf, mittens (clothing easy to put on a puppet) and asks for help getting dressed. He directs you to put clothes on wrong part of his body. Let children help get it right.

QT Participants look at books together.

G Bear paper doll. Copy pattern on plain paper, to be cut out and assembled at home. If covered in plastic and attached to magnets, the bear becomes a toy to be dressed on the refrigerator.

Closing Routine

Notes

Colors

Stories Shared

Brown Bear, Brown Bear, What Do You See?
BILL MARTIN

Mr. Rabbit and the Lovely Present
CHARLOTTE ZOLOTOW

More Stories to Share at Home

Red Light, Green Light
MARGARET WISE BROWN

Calico Cat's Rainbow
DONALD CHARLES

Freight Train
DONALD CREWS

Green Says Go
ED EMBERLEY

Rainbow of My Own
DON FREEMAN

Is It Red? Is It Yellow? Is It Blue?
TANA HOBAN

Colors
JAN PIENKOWSKI

Blue Bug's Book of Colors
VIRGINIA POULET

The Rainbow Mother Goose

Colors
JOHN REISS

My Slippers Are Red
CHARLOTTE STEINER

Grover's Favorite Color
KAY WOOD

Rhythms, Rhymes, and Fingerplays

What Are You Wearing?

(sung to the tune of "Mary Had a Little Lamb")
Martin has a red shirt on . . . *
Red shirt on . . . red shirt on
Martin has a red shirt on
I see him here today!

(*substitute your child's name and clothing)

Traffic Lights

Do you know what traffic lights say to you?
Do you know that traffic lights say to do?
Yellow says, "Be careful!"
Green says, "You may go."
But red is most important,
It says, "Stop!", you know.

Follow-up Ideas

Fingerpaint: This can be messy, so wear an old shirt for a smock and put newspaper under the surface where you'll be working.
To make fingerpaint combine:

1. liquid laundry starch or paste mixed with an equal amount of liquid detergent, and
2. food coloring

Add the food coloring to the starch. Dampen a piece of paper (shelf or butcher paper works best) and drop several teaspoons of fingerpaint on it. Use one or more colors. With your fingers, hands and wrists, swirl the paint around and around, making and changing the designs. Lay it on newspapers to dry.
For temporary art put the paint inside a zip-lock plastic bag and close it. Another idea is to let your toddler paint on a cookie sheet. The results are the same as above but without the mess.

Craft

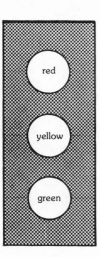

Traffic Light

You will need: black construction paper or felt

green, yellow, and red construction paper or felt

scissors

Cut a 4″×9″ rectangle from the black paper or felt. Using a can or glass as a pattern, draw circles of green, yellow, and red, and cut them out.
Take turns with your toddler putting the colored circles onto the traffic light. As you do, talk about each color and what it means for safety.

Program Notes

Opening Routine	When rearranging the shape puzzle, emphasize colors of the pieces as well as their shapes. Point out colors around the room or in children's clothing.
ST	Display book: *Mr. Rabbit and the Lovely Present.* Use a small basket and artificial fruit (rabbit puppet, optional) to tell the story briefly as you add the fruit to the basket. Leave time after the story for the children to examine the fruit.
A	"What Are You Wearing?" song, sung while standing and clapping hands
ST	Book: *Brown Bear, Brown Bear, What Do You See?*
A	Stretching
ST	Traffic light flannelboard (see above) with "Traffic Lights" rhyme

Sign   "Stop"—Bring edge of right hand down sharply into left palm (like a karate chop).

A   With the traffic light on the flannelboard, have everyone stand and pretend to be a part of the traffic as you call out the lights. Have them follow your lead:

"Green says Go"—move feet quickly, "Go, go, go fast!"

"Yellow says Slow"—move feet slowly, "Go . . . go . . . go slowly."

"Red says Stop!"—stop suddenly.

Repeat several times. Instruct them to "Go slowly" into quiet time activity.

QT   Parent and child look at books together.

G   Colorful stickers or gummed stars

Closing Routine

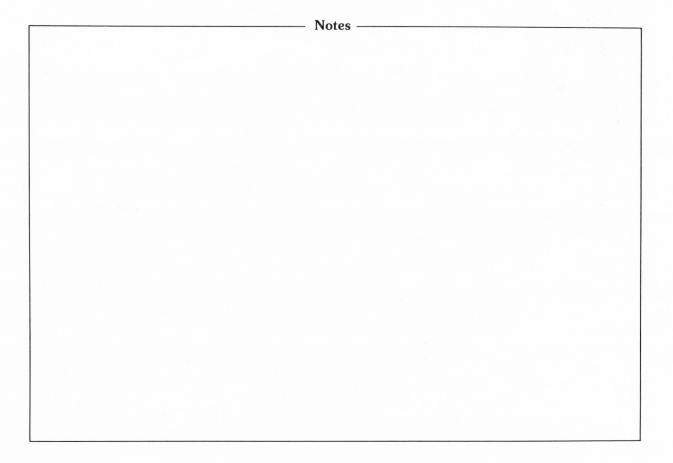

— Notes —

Counting

Stories Shared

Roll Over! A Counting Song
MERLE PEEK

Max's Toys, a Counting Book
ROSEMARY WELLS

More Stories to Share at Home

1, 2, 3 to the Zoo
ERIC CARLE

Counting Rhymes

Kitten from One to Ten
MIRRA GINSBURG

1 Hunter
PAT HUTCHINS

One Rubber Duckie: A Sesame Street Counting Book

Numbers of Things
HELEN OXENBURY

The Chicken Book
GARTH WILLIAMS

Count on Calico Cat
DONALD CHARLES

Chicken Little Count-to-Ten
MARGARET FRISKEY

One, Two, Three, Four, Five
ARTHUR GREGOR

1, 2 Buckle My Shoe
MOTHER GOOSE

Over in the Meadow

Numbers
JAN PIENKOWSKI

Rhythms, Rhymes, and Fingerplays

Inside a Rocket Ship

Inside a rocket ship (crouch down)
Just enough room (hold hands close to body)
Here comes the countdown
1, 2, 3, 4, 5 . . .
Zooooooooommm! (Jump up, throwing hands over head)

Beehive

Here is a beehive, (make fist, cup other hand over it)
Where are the bees?
Hidden away where nobody sees. (peer into fist)
Watch and you'll see them
Come out of the hive, (pull cupped hand away)
1, 2, 3, 4, 5. (extend fingers as counted)
Buzzzzzzzz (flutter fingers)
Bees flying here, bees flying there (flutter fingers)
Bees flying everywhere!
Gathering nectar they fly high and low, (hands high, then low)

They're getting tired and begin to fly slow (flutter fingers slowly)
Back to the hive (slowly pull hands back to first position)
1, 2, 3, 4, 5. Buzzzzzzzzzz (peer into fist)

Follow-up Ideas

Counting: listening to numbers and the sequence in which they come is a good experience for toddlers. Count everything! Don't expect or push your child to count with you. It is the sound and rhythm of the counting that are important and entertaining for them.

Listening to nursery rhymes develops a sense of rhythm in your child. That rhythm is very important in learning to count and read later on.

Craft

Counting Balls

You will need: construction paper or colorful magazine pages

scissors

tape

string, optional

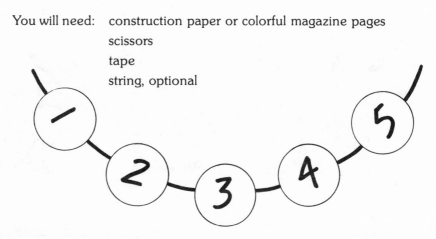

Trace around a glass or bowl to make five circles on different colors of paper. Cut out the circles and number them 1 to 5. Tape them to a door, refrigerator, or wall low enough that your child can touch them, or make a mini-clothesline with a piece of string tied between two objects on which the circles are hung.

Each time you pass them, count the circles. Don't draw too much attention to yourself; just nonchalantly count, "1, 2, 3, 4, 5" and touch each circle as you pass by. Soon your child will be copying this activity and counting, too. Use these circles to talk about colors and line relationships (front, middle, and back).

Program Notes

Opening Routine Count the pieces in the shape puzzle before you assemble them into the clown figure. Point out the "two" stars and ask them to find and count the same on their name tags.

ST Book: *Max's Toys, a Counting Book*

A "Inside a Rocket Ship" action rhyme. Repeat.

ST Display book: *Roll Over!* Flannelboard story with actions. Demonstrate to children the "rolling" motion (moving hands over and around each other) for them to copy during the story.

A Let's count Twos: count things in twos, emphasizing the rhythm and the sequence: One . . . Two. Have children stand and follow your lead as you point out and count: eyes, ears, feet, knees, and so on. Then do actions in twos: 2 hops, 2 big steps, 2 little steps, 2 handclaps, and so on.

ST "Beehive" rhyme using glove puppet with bees

QT Participants look at books together.

G Baby bees bookmark

Closing Routine

— Notes —

Dog-Gone!

Stories Shared

Where's Spot?
ERIC HILL

Who Said Meow?
MARIA POLUSHKIN

More Stories to Share at Home

*Hark, Hark the Dogs Do Bark,
and Other Rhymes...*
LENORE BLEGVAD

The Dog
JOHN BURNINGHAM

Angus and the Cat
MARJORIE FLACK

Claude, the Dog
DICK GACKENBACK

Dogs
JANUSZ GRABIANSKI

Whistle for Willie
EZRA JACK KEATS

Poky Little Puppy
JANETTE S. LOWREY

Old Mother Hubbard and Her Dog
SARAH C. MARTIN

Puppies
JAN PFLOOG

Nothing but Cats and All about Dogs
GRACE M. SKAAR

Very Little Dog
GRACE M. SKAAR

Harry, the Dirty Dog
GENE ZION

Rhythms, Rhymes, and Fingerplays

My Little Dog

Oh where, oh where (look around for dog)
Has my little dog gone?
Oh where, oh where can he be?
With his ears cut short (hand on ears)
And his tail cut long (wag hands behind back)
Oh where, oh where can he be?

Puppy's Doghouse

This is puppy's doghouse (put tips of fingers together)
This is puppy's bed. (hands flat, palms upward)
This is puppy's pan of milk, (cup hands together like bowl)
Where he can be fed.
This is puppy's collar (encircle neck with fingers)
His name is on it, too.
Take a stick and throw it (make throwing motion)
And he'll bring it back to you! (clap hands rapidly)

Follow-up Ideas

Animal alphabet cards can be made with pictures from catalogs, magazines, or greeting cards. Cut out the pictures and glue them to 3″×5″ index cards. Label them boldly with the appropriate alphabet letter. Make an alphabet book using this same idea and typing paper stapled together in book form.

Talk about animal safety to help your child understand caution when meeting unknown pets for the first time without being "introduced." Check with the local animal shelter for guidelines for children to avoid being bitten or frightened of dogs.

Craft

Dog Finger Puppets

You will need: paper

scissors

markers or crayons

tape

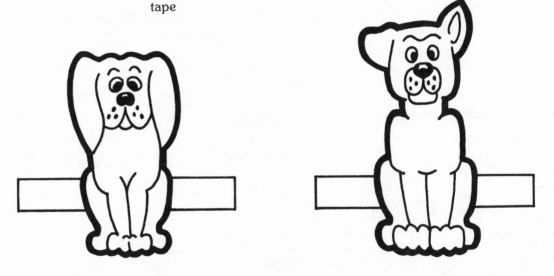

Trace these patterns and cut them out of paper. Color or draw features on them. Wrap the tabs around your child's first and second fingers and tape the ends together. By moving these fingers, the puppies can walk, jump, run, and so on. With a small box you can make a doghouse in which your "pets" can live.

Make additional fingerpuppets by cutting pictures from magazines or greeting cards, leaving tabs on them to wrap around fingers.

Program Notes

Opening Routine   Introduce theme with dog noises (barks, pants, growls) and ask children to guess what the stories are about that day.

Sign   "Dog"—Pat leg with hand, as if calling a dog.

ST   Book: *Who Said Meow?*

A   "My Little Dog" rhyme; afterwards, look for dog and "discover" a dog puppet who likes to be petted, lick noses, and be hugged gently. This puppet precedes the next book to be shared.

ST   Book: *Where's Spot?* Puppet goes out of sight to listen to story.

A   "Puppy's Doghouse" fingerplay

CD   Puppet returns and children make the fingerplay motions as he puts his head in a "doghouse," lies down on a "bed," and so forth. Keep repeating the rhyme until each child has the opportunity to interact with the puppet. Puppet then exits for a nap.

QT   Child and parent look at books together.

G   Puppy ears

Needed: Construction paper; staples; two 10″ pieces of string

Cut a strip of construction paper 2″×6″ and punch a hole at each end; tie a string in each hole. Cut two ears 6″ long; fold under ½″ on flat end. Staple fold to band, behind punched holes. String is tied under child's chin to hold ears in place.

Closing Routine

fold line

6″

ear

—— **Notes** ——

Ducks

Stories Shared

The Little Duck
JUDY DUNN

Three Ducks Went Wandering
RONALD ROY

Other Stories of Interest

Six Little Ducks
CHRIS CONOVER

Angus and the Ducks
MARJORIE FLACK

Story about Ping
MARJORIE FLACK

Seven Diving Ducks
MARGARET FRISKEY

Chick and the Duckling
MIRRA GINSBURG

Make Way for Ducklings
ROBERT MCCLOSKEY

Swim Little Duck
MISKA MILES

Mother Goose

Have You Seen My Duckling?
NANCY TAFURI

Little Wood Duck
BRIAN WILDSMITH

Rhythms, Rhymes, and Fingerplays

The Duck

I waddle when I walk.
(arms elbow high, twist trunk side to side)
I quack when I talk.
(palms together, open and close)
I have webbed toes on my feet.
(fingers spread wide)
Rain coming down
(flutter fingers downward from over head)
Makes me smile, not frown.
(smile)
And I dive for something to eat.
(palms together, diving motion)

I Am a Little Duck

I am a little duck and I go "Quack, quack."
(hands in armpits, flap like wings)
And I wiggle my tail in the back, back, back.
(wiggle backside)
I swim in the water and go "Quack, quack, quack,"
(paddle with hands)
And I wiggle my tail in the back, back, back.
(wiggle backside)

Follow-up Ideas

Make a bank: Use empty cans with plastic lids (such as those that potato chips or tennis balls come in). Cover the can with fabric or paper and glue on pictures cut from magazines or photographs of your child. Cut a slot in the plastic lid and let your child drop money into the bank. Supervise children with coins closely, so they don't swallow them.

Make a baby scrapbook including pieces of discarded favorite toys, clothes, photographs, blankets, and so on, just for your child. She or he will enjoy looking and touching familiar parts of the past. Talk about these things and their relationship to your child.

Craft

Little Duck Salad

You will need: a plate

1 leaf of lettuce

½ of a canned pear, slice lengthwise

2 raisins

1 slice of cheese, cut into 2 small triangles and three ovals (2 large and 1 small)

2 short carrot sticks

Lay the lettuce on the plate and arrange the pear and other foods to resemble a duck in this way:

Pear, small end at top (head and body)
Raisins (eyes)
Cheese: triangles (webbed feet)
          ovals (wings and beak)
Carrot sticks (legs)

This healthy snack is great fun, too!

Program Notes

Opening Routine	Introduce theme with puppet wearing a duck headband and making quacking noises.
Sign	"Duck"—Thumb, index finger, and middle finger form beak which opens and closes near mouth.
ST	Book: *Three Ducks Went Wandering*
A	"I Am a Little Duck" action rhyme. Repeat.
ST	Book: *The Little Duck*
A	"The Duck" fingerplay
P	Puppet returns with duck headbands for all children. Put them on and repeat rhyme "I Am a Little Duck." Lead a duck parade around the storyspace, ending with little ducks settling into their parents' nests (arms).
QT	Participants look at books together.
G	Duck headbands

Needed: Construction paper; staples; marker

Cut a 2"×18" strip of construction paper for each headband. Mark the center and staple eyes and duck's bill on headband as shown. Overlap headband ends and staple together. Headband is worn on the child's forehead.

Closing Routine	"Ducks" parade, flapping wings and quacking as they exit storyspace.

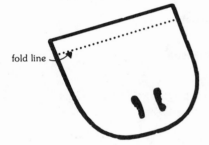

fold line

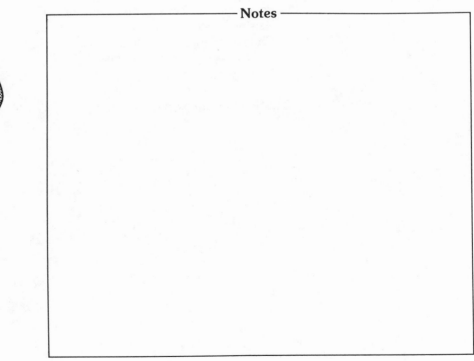

── **Notes** ──

3½"

Farms

Stories Shared

Farm Animals
LISA BONFORTE

Old MacDonald Had a Farm

More Stories to Share at Home

I Know a Farm
ETHEL COLLIER

The Little Farm
LOIS LENSKI

To Market, To Market
MOTHER GOOSE

Our Animal Friends
ALICE PROVENSEN AND
MARTIN PROVENSEN

Wake Up Farm
ALVIN TRESSELT

Flip and the Cows
WESLEY DENNIS

Boo to a Goose
JOSEPH LOW

Who Took the Farmer's Hat?
JOAN NODSET

Animals on the Farm
FEODOR S. ROJANKOVSKY

If I Drove a Tractor
MIRIAM YOUNG

Petunia
ROGER ANTOINE DUVOISIN

Friendly Farm Animals
ESTHER MEEKS

Morning
MARIA POLUSHKIN

Farm Numbers 1, 2, 3
DONALD SMITH

Farmer in the Dell
DIANE ZUROMSKIA

Rhythms, Rhymes, and Fingerplays

Here Is a Farmer

Here is a farmer,
What does he do?
He feeds the cows
And milks them, too.
  Chickens and pigs,
  Horses and sheep,
  He puts in the barn
  To eat and sleep.

He drives the tractor,
Fields to sow.
Plants the seeds
So they will grow.
  Here is the farmer,
  At work or play.
  He keeps busy
  All through the day.

The Scarecrow

The old scarecrow is a funny old man.
He flaps in the wind as hard as he can.
He flaps to the right, (lean right)
He flaps to the left, (lean left)
He flaps back and forth (lean forward and back)
'Til he's 'most out of breath.
His arms swing out (swing arms)
His legs swing, too. (swing legs)
He nods his head (nod head)
"How do you do?"
See him flippity flop (swing arms and legs)
When the wind blows hard,
That old scarecrow
In our backyard.

Follow-up Ideas

Make animal sounds as a game or when singing "Old MacDonald Had a Farm." Some fun sounds are:

chicken (cluck)	dog (bow-wow)	duck (quack)
pig (oink)	cat (meow)	lamb (baa)
bird (chirp)	horse (neigh)	lion (roar)
donkey (hee-haw)	crow (caw)	snake (hiss)
rooster (cock-a-doodle-doo)		

Sing together when doing routines like dressing, bathing, or waiting. Sing nursery rhymes or favorite songs. Play your favorite phonograph record and dance. Try to dance fast, slow, and sitting down.

Craft

Old Scarecrow Flannelboard

You will need: felt pieces
scissors
markers

Cut the following pieces from different colors of felt:

1 stick, the length of the scarecrow
1 pair pants
1 shirt
2 hands
1 hat
1 circle, for head

Draw a face on the circle and make patches, buttons, and pockets on the shirt and pants. Assemble the pieces, beginning with the stick and ending with the hat, using a flannelboard or a cushion from the sofa. Recite "The Scarecrow" rhyme with your child and act out the motions.

Program Notes

Opening Routine   Storyteller or puppet wears a straw hat and introduces the theme.

ST   Book: *Farm Animals*

A   "Here Is a Farmer" action rhyme

ST   Display book: *Old MacDonald Had a Farm.* Distribute animal stick puppets to children who may hold them up and make animal sounds at the appropriate time in the song. Use only five animals.

A   "Farm animals" march around storyspace following the "farmer" who leads them to the barn (touchbox). Children put their animals in the barn.

ST   Scarecrow flannelboard (see above). Assemble one piece at a time from the stick up and describe how scarecrows keep birds from eating the seeds planted in the fields.

Sign   "Scarecrow"—Spread fingers wide; hold hands in front of chest, palms in, fingers pointing at each other. Move hands toward each other in two quick, jerky motions (a scaring motion). Index finger and thumb form beak which opens and closes near mouth (bird).

A   "The Scarecrow" action rhyme

QT   Parent and child look at books together.

G   Farm animal fingerpuppets. Copy, tape flaps together, and give one to each child.

Closing Routine

— Notes —

Food

Stories Shared

Is This My Dinner?
IRMA SIMONTON BLACK

Pancakes, Pancakes
ERIC CARLE

*I Know an Old Lady Who
Swallowed a Fly: A Folksong*

More Stories to Share at Home

The Fish
DICK BRUNA

The Cupboard
JOHN BURNINGHAM

Very Hungry Caterpillar
ERIC CARLE

*Pease Porridge Hot, a Mother
Goose Cookbook*
LORINDA CAULEY

Pancakes for Breakfast
TOMIE dePAOLA

Gingerbread Boy

*Everybody Has a House and
Everybody Eats*
MARY MCBURNEY GREEN

*Little Red Hen and the Grain of
Wheat*

Blueberries for Sal
ROBERT MCCLOSKEY

Great Big Enormous Turnip
ALEKSEI TOLSTOY

Autumn Harvest
ALVIN TRESSELT

Winter Picnic
ROBERT WELBER

Rhythms, Rhymes, and Fingerplays

The Apple Tree

Away up high in the apple tree (point up)
Two red apples smiled at me. (point to self)
I shook that tree as hard as I could, (shaking motion)
And down they came . . . (point down)
Mmmmm, they were good! (rub tummy)

Doughnut

Here is a doughnut
(form circle with thumbs and forefingers)
Round and fat.
There's a hole in the middle
(hold finger-circle up and look through it)
But you can't eat that!! (shake head)

Pancake

Mix a pancake, (stirring motions)
Stir a pancake,
Pop it in the pan. (pouring motion)
Fry the pancake, (like you're holding a skillet)
Toss the pancake, (throwing motion)
Catch it if you can. (catching motion)

(Christine Rossetti)

Follow-up Ideas

Cut pictures of food from magazines or can labels and glue them on index cards to make a card matching game. To make a food scrapbook, glue the pictures to typing or notebook paper and staple the edges together. Try to find pictures of your child's favorite foods.

Try fun recipes for easy treats like peanut butter sandwiches with banana slices, or yogurt with fruit or jelly mixed in, or invent your own with favorite foods. Let your child help assemble ingredients while you watch or help.

Craft

Finger-Tasting Sock Puppet

You will need: an old sock with toe and heel intact
needle and thread
notions for features (buttons, pom-poms, yarn)

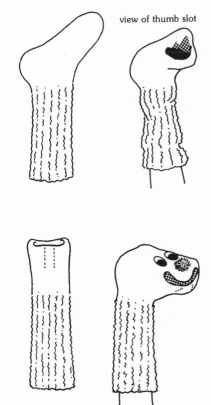

view of thumb slot

Place the sock over your hand with the heel over your knuckles. Open your fingers wide inside the sock and tuck the toe into the palm of your hand. With needle and thread, sew the underside of the sock "mouth," forming a slot into which your thumb can slide.

Sew on eyes keeping them close to the mouth opening. Add nose, hair, clothes . . . whatever you want to make the puppet real. Please, no teeth, however. Keep the puppet non-threatening. Features can be made with any scraps or odds and ends you have around. Avoid using materials which cannot be washed. The puppet can be thrown in the laundry with the family clothes.

Sock puppets are very flexible, "make faces" easily, and can be used by either adults or children. Practice moving your fingers inside the puppet to make happy faces, sad faces, and silly faces.

To taste fingers: Have the puppet gently suck or lick the fingers of children with a slurping sound, and then tell each child what his or her finger tasted like. Use flavors with which the children are familiar.

Program Notes

**Opening
Routine**

Sign "Eat"—With the thumb and fingers together, tap mouth twice.

ST Book: *Pancakes, Pancakes*

A "Pancake" fingerplay

ST Book: *Is This My Dinner?*

CD Getting ready for dinner: Act out feeling hungry, washing hands, setting table (put felt shapes on flannelboard for place setting—see giveaway below), eating, drinking, and washing dishes.

ST *I Know an Old Lady Who Swallowed a Fly.* Use sack puppet of "old lady" with window stomach.

A Stretching

QT Parent and child look at books together.

G Placemat (and flannelboard figures)

Needed: White and colored construction paper; glue; marker

Trace around a small plate, glass, spoon, and fork for patterns. Cut them from white paper and glue to colored paper as shown. With a marker, print child's name on top of placemat. Laminate, if possible, or parent may cover it with clear contact paper. For flannelboard, cut shapes from felt.

**Closing
Routine**

┌─────────────────── **Notes** ───────────────────┐
│   │
│   │
│   │
│   │
│   │
│   │
│   │
│   │
└──┘

Frogs and Turtles

Stories Shared

Turtle Tale
FRANK ASCH

Jump, Frog, Jump
ROBERT KALAN

More Stories to Share at Home

Clever Turtle
ROSLYN ABISCH

Turtle
BETTY SUE CUMMINGS

Bert and Barney
NED DELANEY

The Hare and the Tortoise
JEAN DE LA FONTAINE

Turtle and the Monkey
PAUL GALDONE

Frogs Merry
JULIET KEPES

Tadpole and the Frog
SUSAN KNOBLER

Mert the Blurt
ROBERT KRAUS

Voices of Greenwillow Pond
CAROLYN LANE

Theodor Turtle
ELLEN MACGREGOR

Jump, Frog, Jump
PATRICIA MILES MARTIN

A Boy, a Dog and a Frog
MERCER MAYER

Toad
ANNE ROCKWELL AND
HARLOW ROCKWELL

Foolish Frog
PETE SEEGER

Rhythms, Rhymes, and Fingerplays

The Little Frog

I am a little frog (squat down)
Hopping on a log. (bounce up and down)
Listen to my song. ("ribbit, ribbit")
I sleep all winter long. (lay head against hands)
Wake up and peek out (peek between fingers)
Up I jump, all about. (bounce up and down)
I catch flies (grabbing motion)
I wink my eyes (blink)
I hop and hop (bounce up and down)
And then I stop. (sit down on floor)

Little Turtle

There was a little turtle (make fist, cover with other hand)
Who lived in a box. (both hands, fingers touching)
He swam in the water, (thumbs together, flutter fingers)
And climbed on the rocks. ("walk" one hand over the other)
He snapped at a mosquito, (grabbing motion, up high)
He snapped at a flea, (grabbing motion, in front)
He snapped at a minnow, (grabbing motion, down low)
And he snapped at me! (grabbing motion, under chin)
He caught the mosquito, (clap hands up high)
He caught the flea, (clap hands in front)
He caught the minnow, (clap hands down low)
But he didn't catch me! (point to self, shake head)

(Vachel Lindsay)

Follow-up Ideas

Teach your child to play Leap Frog. Have your child crouch low on the floor and then jump over him or her. You then crouch low and the child hops (or climbs) over you. Play in a carpeted area so falls are softened. Leap in a circle or from one point to another (sofa to door).

Make a "turtle" salad for lunch using peach halves for its shell, a nut or marshmallow for a head, and carrot sticks for legs and a tail.

Craft

Turtle Marionette

You will need: a plastic bowl
construction paper
crayons or markers
scissors
glue
button
string

Let your child decorate the bowl which will become the turtle's shell. Cut from construction paper: 1 circle (head), 4 small rectangles (legs), and 1 triangle (tail). Draw a face on the circle and glue the paper shapes to the edge of the bowl.

Poke a hole in the center of the bowl and thread the string through it. Thread the button onto the string and tie securely. This helps to keep the string from pulling out of the bowl.

Hold the string, and the turtle will dangle above the floor. He can be made to walk slowly, hop, dance, or even fly.

Program Notes

Opening Routine

Sign	"Turtle"—Cup left hand over right fist. Extend right thumb and wiggle it, like turtle peeking from under shell.
ST	Book: *Turtle Tale*
A	"Little Turtle" fingerplay
ST	Display book: *Jump, Frog, Jump* (flannelboard story)
A	"The Little Frog" action rhyme
CD	Review *Jump, Frog, Jump*, having each child be a frog and jump when you say, "Jump, frog, jump!"
QT	Child and parent look at books together.

G Frog puppet

Needed: Letter-sized envelopes; construction paper; glue

Fold envelope in half, short ends together. On front side cut a slit along the fold. Glue flap down in back. Cut out eyes and body, and fold on lines. Attach eyes to one side of envelope and body to the other. Insert hand into slit to make mouth open and close.

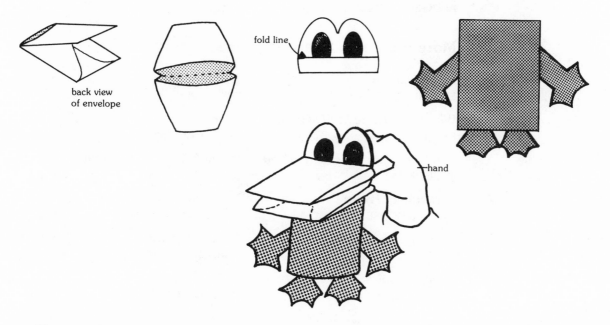

back view
of envelope

fold line

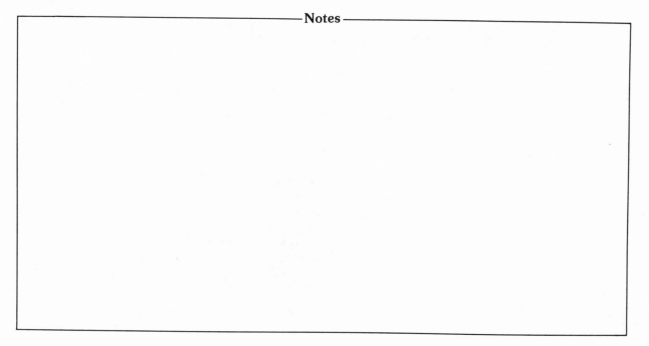

hand

Closing Routine   Have children hop out of storyspace like frogs.

── **Notes** ──

Gardens

Stories Shared

The Carrot Seed
RUTH KRAUSS

The Great Big Enormous Turnip
ALEKSEI TOLSTOY

The Little Red Hen and the Grain of Wheat

More Stories to Share at Home

In the Garden
EUGENE BOOTH

Who Goes There in My Garden?
ETHEL COLLIER

The Seed That Peacock Planted
JULIET KEPES

Pocketful of Posies
MOTHER GOOSE

How My Garden Grew
ANNE F. ROCKWELL

Time for Flowers
MARK TAYLOR

The Tiny Seed
ERIC CARLE

Titch
PAT HUTCHINS

Buzzy Bear in the Garden
DOROTHY MARINO

A Zoo in My Garden
CHIUOKO NAKATANI

Compost Heap
HAROLD ROCKWELL

In My Garden
CHARLOTTE ZOLOTOW

Rhythms, Rhymes, and Fingerplays

My Garden

This is my garden
(hands in front, palms up)
I'll rake it with care
(rake fingers of one hand over other palm)
And then some flower seeds
(twist index finger of one hand into center of palm)
I will plant there.
(pat palm with other fingers)

The sun will shine
(make circle with arms over head)
And the rain will fall,
(wiggle fingers down in front of body)
And my garden will blossom
(make fists, open fingers slowly)
Growing straight and tall.
(reach hands high above head)

I Dig, Dig, Dig

I dig, dig, dig (digging motion)
And I plant some seeds. (planting motion)
I rake, rake, rake (raking motion)
And I pull some weeds. (pulling motion)
I wait and watch (hands on hips)
And soon I know, (point to self)
My garden sprouts (hands low, palms down)
And starts to grow. (raise hands toward ceiling)

Follow-up Ideas

Plant seeds from the fruits you eat, such as oranges, grapefruits, tangerines, or lemons. Rinse the seeds and blot them dry with a paper towel. Plant in a container filled with potting soil, labeling which pot is which. Put the pots in a warm place and water daily. When shoots begin to appear, move them to a sunny window, and keep the soil moist.

Make a sponge planter with a piece of natural (not man-made) sponge. Soak the sponge in water; then sprinkle with grass seed or birdseed. Hang with a string in a sunny window and soak the sponge every day. Soon it will be filled with lovely green plants.

Talk about things that grow in gardens while in the grocery store. The produce department is an ideal place to start, with fresh vegetables and fruits, but also point out that some canned products also begin as seeds. Give each item a name as you pass it, building your child's vocabulary. If you don't know, ask the attendant. It's fun to learn new foods!

Craft

Funny Potato Face

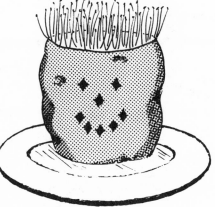

You will need: 1 large raw potato

cotton balls

grass seed or birdseed

a knife and a tablespoon

a few whole cloves

a small dish of water

Scoop some of the pulp out of the top of the potato. Moisten the cotton with water and place it in the hollow of the potato. Slice off the bottom of the potato so it will stand by itself; place in the dish of water. Let your child sprinkle the seed over the cotton. Stick the cloves in the side of the potato to make eyes, nose, and mouth. Keep the cotton moist and in a few days the potato will sprout a wonderful head of green hair!

Program Notes

Opening Routine

ST Display book: *The Little Red Hen* (flannelboard story)

A "My Garden" fingerplay

ST Display book: *The Great Big Enormous Turnip* (glove puppet story). Have children make pulling motions during the story as characters try to pull up the turnip.

A "I Dig, Dig, Dig" action rhyme

ST Book: *The Carrot Seed*

CD Puppet brings out Garden Box (with giant carrot inside). Act out *The Carrot Seed* using a toy rake and watering can. Children can pretend to plant the carrot seed, water it, rake it, and when it sprouts (feather duster inserted), help the storyteller to pull it up. As in *The Great Big Enormous Turnip*, the effort should involve several tries before it is successful. Leave time for them to look at and touch the carrot after it is "harvested."

QT Parent and child look at books together.

G Carrot seeds

Needed: Purchased carrot seeds; small envelopes

Divide a packet of seeds into small, sealed envelopes. Staple a copy of instructions to each envelope. Keep a few out to put in a plastic bag so children can see how small they are. Stress that the envelope should not be opened until they get home so the seeds won't get lost. Have the puppet distribute seeds.

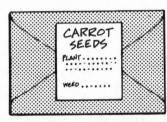

Closing Routine

Note

Boo! (Halloween)

Stories Shared

Humbug Witch
LORNA BALIAN

One Dark Night
EDNA MITCHELL PRESTON

More Stories to Share at Home

Woggle of Witches
ADRIENNE ADAMS

Three Billy Goats Gruff
PETER CHRISTEN ASBJORNSEN

Georgie
ROBERT BRIGHT

Dark, Dark Tale
RUTH BROWN

In a Pumpkin Shell, a Mother Goose ABC

There's a Nightmare in My Closet
MERCER MAYER

Mousekin's Golden House
EDNA MILLER

Meg and Mog
HELEN NICOLL

Where the Wild Things Are
MAURICE SENDAK

Teeny-Tiny Woman
BARBARA SEULING

Pleasant Fieldmouse's Halloween Party
JAN WAHL

Rhythms, Rhymes, and Fingerplays

Jack-O-Lantern

Carve a jack-o-lantern on Halloween night.
(hand open, thumb on top, make sawing motion)
He has a big mouth, but he doesn't bite.
(index fingers pull up corners of mouth)
He has two big eyes, but he cannot see.
(hands encircle eyes like spectacles)
He's a funny jack-o-lantern,
(hands on stomach, rock back and forth, laughing)
As happy as can be.

Two Little Ghosts

A very old witch was stirring a pot,
(make stirring motion)
Ooo-oooo! Ooo-oooo!
Two little ghosts said, "What has she got?"
(shrug shoulders)
Tippytoe, tippytoe, tippytoe . . .
("walk" fingers up arm or tiptoe in circle)
Boo!
(clap hands sharply)

Follow-up Ideas

Keep a "dress-up box" filled with old clothes, hats, scarves, shoes, and handbags for children to use while pretending.

Paper bag costumes are fun and economical. Two books to help you with ideas and construction of them are: Betsy Pflug, *Funny Bags* and Goldie T. Chernoff, *Easy Costumes You Don't Have to Sew.*

Craft

Wild Thing Sack Puppet

You will need: small paper sack (lunch sized or smaller)
glue
scraps of material, paper, yarn, felt
crayons or magic markers
pipe cleaners, trim, buttons

Using the bottom flap of the paper bag as the face of your puppet, draw or glue on it features that appear on the upper half of the face: eyes, brows, nose, cheeks, mustache. Under the flap of the bag, draw the mouth so that it is visible only when the flap is raised. Add tongue, lips, and chin. Use teeth sparingly.

Decorate the rest of the bag with your scraps and odds and ends, using glue. Let glue dry thoroughly.

To operate, place sack over the hand and move the flap (mouth) up and down as the puppet talks.

Program Notes

Before Program Invite children to attend in costume. Have jack-o-lantern (or pumpkin on which a face will be drawn) on display.

Opening Routine Spend time examining each other's costumes. Some children may be frightened of others in strange garb. A puppet wearing a costume will usually reassure them. Have those wearing masks or cumbersome attachments remove them before beginning the stories.

Sign "Halloween"—Cover face with hands; slowly move them to the sides of the face, as if you were removing a mask.

ST Display book: *One Dark Night.* Lap stage story using stand-up figures.

A "Two Little Ghosts" fingerplay. Start by saying "Boo" together to avoid startling anyone. Then practice the sequence "tippytoe, tippytoe, Boo!" a couple of times so they will know it is coming in the rhyme.

ST   Display book: *Humbug Witch* (flannelboard story). The figure starts off with the mask and wig already in place. This makes the removal of them at the end a delightful surprise.

P   Talk about the pumpkin and how it gets its face. If not carved, draw a face on the pumpkin with a marker.

A   "Jack-O-Lantern" fingerplay

QT   Participants look at books together.

G   Tissue ghosts

Needed: white facial tissues; cotton balls or lollipops; tape; marker

Lay tissue flat on table. Place cotton ball in its center. Gather tissue around the cotton ball and tape in place. Draw on eyes.

Lollipops are good because their sticks are ready-made handles, but check with parents first to see if all can have sweets.

Closing Routine

Notes

Hats

Stories Shared

Martin's Hats
JOAN BLOS

Caps for Sale
ESPHYR SLOBODKINA

More Stories to Share at Home

The Wind Thief
JUDI BARRETT

500 Hats of Bartholomew Cubbins
THEODOR SEUSS GEISEL

Paddy's New Hat
JOHN GOODALL

Benny's Four Hats
RUTH JAYNES

Jenny's Hat
EZRA JACK KEATS

Animal Hat Shop
SARA MURPHY

Who Took the Farmer's Hat?
JOAN L. NODSET

My Closet Full of Hats
HARVEY WEISS

The Cap That Mother Made
CHRISTINE WESTERBERGER

The Horse in the Easter Bonnet
CATHERINE WOOLLEY

Rhythms, Rhymes, and Fingerplays

Hats

A cowboy wears a cowboy hat (hands encircle head)
As he gallops on his horse. (galloping motion)
A fireman's hat keeps him safe (hands encircle head)
As fires run their course. (spraying motion as with hose)
A clown wears a pointy hat (hands form point on head)
And a smile upon his face. (smile broadly)
And astronauts wear helmets, (encircle face with hands)
When blasting into space. (palms together, shoot hands up to sky)

Paper Hat

Fold the paper, first in half,
Turn corners down. Now don't you laugh!
Turn up the edges, this way and that.
Now put it on. It's a paper hat!

Follow-up Ideas

Save the Sunday comics and make paper hats for your toddler and special playfellows (toys and other friends). This is a quick and inexpensive diversion that is fun on rainy days. Decorate hats with paper scraps, crayons, feathers, and so on.

Try to find pictures of many different kinds of hats in magazines or catalogs. Mount them on index cards to make them more durable, and let your child "put hats on" people in pictures in other books. Talk about different kinds of hats, who wears them, and the act of putting them "on" and taking them "off." Keep your hat collection in a plastic margarine "hat box."

Craft

Helmets

You will need: plastic milk gallon jug, washed thoroughly

scissors and packing knife

adhesive or cloth tape

glue

markers, cloth, and paper scraps

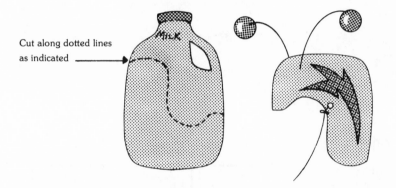

Cut along dotted lines as indicated ⟶

Cut the milk jug in one continuous movement, removing the spout and lid, handle, and bottom of jug. What is left is a piece of bowl-shaped plastic that will form the body of the helmet. Place over your child's head and mark where it should be cut away so it does not rub against shoulders, ears, or neck. You may have to stuff a small towel inside it to make it sit right on your child's head. Cover the edges with tape to avoid scratches.

When the helmet fits comfortably, decorate it with markers or scraps to create a motorcycle, football, or astronaut helmet.

Program Notes

Opening Routine   Have different kinds of hats on display.

Sign   "Hat"—Pat top of head with right hand.

ST   Book: *Martin's Hats*

A   "Hats" fingerplay

P   Have the puppet try on different hats and talk about who wears them and when. Let children try them on if they want.

ST   Book: *Caps for Sale*

CD   Act out *Caps for Sale* with the storyteller acting as peddler and the children as monkeys who copy the peddler's actions. Use small plastic bowls for caps. When finished, have children return caps to touchbox.

P   Have the puppet bring a piece of newspaper and ask the storyteller to fold a paper hat. Fold the hat and put it on puppet. Puppet goes off wearing the new hat.

QT   Participants look at books together.

G   Paper hats. Fold from newspaper or butcher paper. Child's name can be printed on front of the hat. Puppet distributes them to children.

Closing Routine

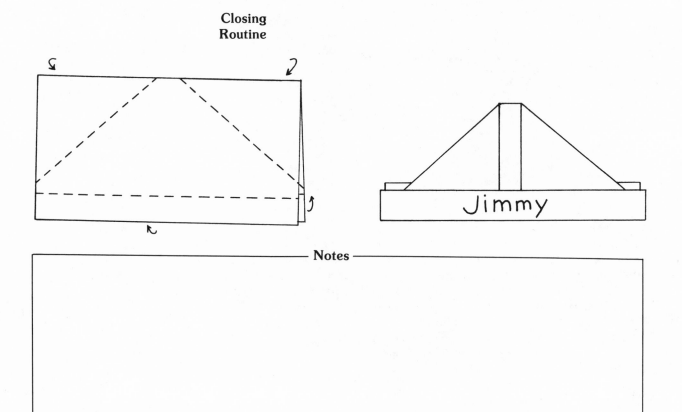

— Notes —

74

Homes

Stories Shared

A House Is a House for Me
MARY ANN HOBERMAN

Homes
JAN PIENKOWSKI

More Stories to Share at Home

Benedict Finds a Home
CHRIS DEMAREST

Everybody Has a House
MARY M. GREEN

The House That Jack Built

Biggest House in the World
LEO LIONNI

Great Big Animal Book
FEODOR ROJANKOVSKY

Homes
CHRISTINE SHARR

In a People House
THEODOR SEUSS GEISEL

How We Live
ANITA HARPER

Sara and the Door
VIRGINIA JENSEN

Door to Door
MAUREEN ROFFEY

My House
MIRIAM SCHLEIN

Oh, Were They Ever Happy
PETER SPIER

Rhythms, Rhymes, and Fingerplays

Houses

This is a nest for Mr. Bluebird
(cup hand palm up to form nest)
This is a hive for Mr. Bee
(close fist for hive)
This is the hole for Bunny Rabbit,
(with fingers of both hands form circle)
And this is a house for me!
(fingers form a peaked roof shape over head)

I Shut the Door

I shut the door and locked it tight,
(clap hands together)
And put the key out of sight.
(pretend to put key in pocket)
I found the key to open the door
(pull out key and hold out in front)
And turned, and turned, and turned some more . . .
(make turning motions)
And then . . . I opened the door!
("open" hands in front of body)

Follow-up Ideas

Make paper puppets: Cut pictures from old magazines or photographs of people, animals, and objects. Tape the pictures to the end of a popsicle stick leaving enough room at the other end to hold the stick. These stick puppets can be used to talk about different kinds of homes, to make up stories, or to act out feelings.

Children need to learn the different names for places where people live. Point out houses, apartment buildings, trailers, motels, and other places as you travel in the car.

Use different-sized cereal, detergent, and other boxes to create a village of your own. Cut out doors and windows so that small animal and people figures can be placed in their homes.

Craft

Bird Feeder

You will need: peanut butter
a styrofoam cup
piece of string
bird seed

Tie a knot in one end of the string. Make a small hole in the bottom of the cup and thread the string through the hole with the knot on the inside. Cover the cup, inside and out, with peanut butter and roll it in bird seed until it is well covered.

Hang the cup outside near a window so you can watch the birds eat!

Program Notes

Opening Routine

Sign "House"—Peak hands over the head. Move them out to the side and down like a roof.

ST Book: *A House Is a House for Me*

A "Houses" fingerplay

ST Book: *Homes*

A "I Shut the Door" fingerplay

ST Homes (flannelboard story). Display different kinds of homes on flannelboard and match pictures of people and animals to where they live:
House/Apartment—People, pets
Barn—Farm animals

Tree—Birds, squirrels
Pond—Fish, frogs, turtles
Hole—Rabbit, mouse

A Stretching

QT Parent and child look at books together.

G Keys bookmark. Copy and distribute, to be mounted on cardboard, cut out, and strung on string at home.

**Closing
Routine**

─── **Notes** ───

Kittens

Stories Shared

Mittens for Kittens, and Other Rhymes about Cats
LENORE BLEVGAD

Will That Wake Mother?
MARTHA M. WELCH

Have You Seen My Cat?
ERIC CARLE

More Stories to Share at Home

Angus and the Cat
MARJORIE FLACK

Three Kittens
MIRRA GINSBURG

One Little Kitten
TANA HOBAN

Come Here Cat
JOAN M. LEXAU

Meg's Eggs
HELEN NICOLL

Nothing But Cats and All About Dogs
GRACE SKAAR

Millions of Cats
WANDA GAG

Cats
JANUSZ GRABIANSKI

Winter Cat
HOWARD C. KNOTTS

Kittens ABC
CLARE T. NEWBERRY

Kittens
JAN PFLOOG

Rhythms, Rhymes, and Fingerplays

Kitten Is Hiding

A kitten is hiding under a chair.
(crouch low, hands over head to hide)
I looked and looked for her everywhere.
(stand, peer around room)
Under the table and under the bed,
(look down)
I looked in the corner and when I said,
(turn around)
"Come kitty, come kitty, here's milk for you,"
(crouch low, hands cupped in front to make dish)
Kitty came running and calling, "Mew, mew, mew."
(scamper on all fours, calling "Mew")

Five Little Kittens

One, two, three, four, five. (hold up fingers and count them)
Five little kittens standing in a row.
They nod their heads to the children, so. (bend fingers)
They run to the left (wiggle fingers left)
They run to the right. (wiggle fingers right)
They stand and stretch in the bright sunlight. (stretch fingers wide)
Along comes a dog (move other hand close to fingers)
Looking for some fun.
Meowwww!
See those kittens run! (hands go behind back)

Follow-up Ideas

Trace your child's hands and feet on a paper sack. Cut the tracings out and hang them where they can be admired. Tape a hand onto cupboards or drawers where your children's toys or clothes are kept as an indication that they can get into these areas by themselves.

If your toddlers are being uncooperative, try chanting as you help them do what you want them to: "I'm putting on your shoe, shoe, shoe, shoe. . . ." This seems to ease stubbornness.

Craft

Yummy Gelly Animals

You will need: 2 envelopes of unflavored gelatin

2 small boxes of flavored gelatin (with or without sugar)

1½ cups cold water

1½ cups hot water

flat cake pan or cookie sheet with sides

cookie cutters

covered container for storage

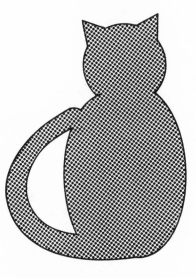

Dissolve the unflavored gelatin in the cold water. Add the hot water to the flavored gelatin and stir until dissolved. Add to cold water mixture and stir until dissolved.

Pour into a flat cake pan or cookie sheets with rims. Chill in refrigerator until firm, then cut with cookie cutters to make animals and shapes (or cut gelatin into blocks with a knife). Save all the scraps to nibble on later.

Store in a covered container in the refrigerator. Although it is as wiggly as traditional Jello, it is easier to handle with fingers and fun to eat. Use some caution when your child is eating gelly animals; the coloring may stain some fabrics.

Program Notes

Opening Routine Introduce program with meows and purrs and have children guess the theme. A cat puppet can also be used.

Sign "Cat"—Pinch thumb and index finger together beside nose as if pulling a cat's whiskers.

ST Book: *Have You Seen My Cat?*

A "Kitten Is Hiding" action rhyme

ST Display book: *Mittens for Kittens* (flannelboard of the rhyme "The Three Little Kittens Have Lost Their Mittens")

CD Act out *Mittens for Kittens* with children being kittens, meowing, seeking, and finding their mittens, and sharing pie with mother.

ST Book: *Will That Wake Mother?* Cat puppet can help decide the answer ("yes" or "no").

A "Five Little Kittens" fingerplay

QT Participants look at books together.

G Kitten mask

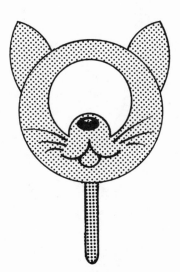

Needed: Paper plates; scissors; marker and staples; wooden ice cream stick

Cut a 4″ circle from center of plates. Cut two ears from the circle and staple to top of plate. Attach the wooden stick so children can hold mask in front of their face while they peek through the center.

Closing Routine

Notes

I Love You!

Stories Shared

Just like Daddy
FRANK ASCH

Ask Mr. Bear
MARJORIE FLACK

More Stories to Share at Home

Are You My Mother?
P. D. EASTMAN

A Pocket for Corduroy
DON FREEMAN

Who Needs Me?
FLORENCE P. HEIDE

Snuggle Bunny
NANCY JEWELL

Bundle Book
RUTH KRAUSS

Just for You
MERCER MAYER

One I Love, Two I Love
MOTHER GOOSE

On Mother's Lap
ANN H. SCOTT

The Daddy Book
ROBERT STEWART

Catch Me, Kiss Me, Say It Again
CLYDE WATSON

I Love My Mother
PAUL ZINDEL

Hold My Hand
CHARLOTTE ZOLOTOW

Rhythms, Rhymes, and Fingerplays

Make a Valentine

Snip, snip, snip the paper.
(slide palms of hand up and down like blades of scissors)
Paste, paste, paste the paper.
(brush fingers against palm of other hand)
Press, press, press the paper.
(press palms together)
To make a valentine for you!
(make "giving" motion)

I Have a Little Heart

I have a little heart (hand over heart)
And it goes thump, thump, thump (pat chest with fingers)
It keeps right on beating
When I jump, jump, jump. (jump in place)
I get a special feeling (hug shoulders)
When I look at you. (point to children)
It makes me want to give you (shrug shoulders shyly)
A kiss or two! (storyteller blows kisses to child, parent kisses child on cheek)

Follow-up Ideas

My own mailbox: Everyone loves to get mail, and toddlers love to put things into a container and dump them out again. To make a mailbox for your toddler, you will need:

a box with a lid (shoe boxes are ideal)

crayons, paint, photos, and so on, to decorate it

"letters" (junk mail, old greeting cards, or postcards)

Cut a slot in the lid of the box and decorate it colorfully. It is now ready to receive "mail." Toddlers also like to put their "treasures" in these boxes, so make the slot a little wider than needed for mail.

Everyone likes to know they are loved. Tell your child often that you care. Touching is also an important way to show your feelings: hugs, kisses, and loving strokes are essential.

Craft

I-Love-You Bookmark

You will need: a photograph (that can be cut)

scissors

a 6″ piece of ribbon or colored paper

glue

felt-tipped marking pen

Cut the photograph into the shape of a heart with the person's face in the center of the heart. Glue the heart-photo to one end of the ribbon and let dry thoroughly.

With a marking pen, write a special message on the bookmark like "I Love You," "Best Grandma," "Big Sister," or the name of the person in the picture or the one receiving the bookmark.

Program Notes

**Opening
Routine**

Sign   "Love"—Cross arms over chest with hands on shoulders, like a hug.

  ST   Display book: *Ask Mr. Bear* (flannelboard story)

  A   Bear puppet gives hugs to each child. Children give hugs to their parents.

  ST   Book: *Just like Daddy*

A Make a valentine. Fold a piece of construction paper and cut a heart shape from it. Let each child help decorate the valentine with a crayon. When finished, call the puppet and have one or two children give the valentine to it. The puppet thanks each child and takes the valentine back to his hiding place.

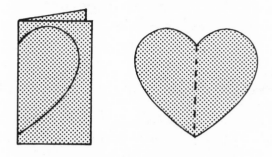

A "I Have a Little Heart" action rhyme

QT Parent and child look at books together.

G Valentines. Either purchased or made from construction paper as above, these are distributed to the children by the puppet before they leave the storyspace.

Closing Routine

Notes

Me

Stories Shared

My Feet Do
JEAN HOLZENTHALER

My Hands Can
JEAN HOLZENTHALER

I Did It
HARLOW ROCKWELL

More Stories to Share at Home

Is This My Dinner?
IRMA S. BLACK

Frances the Face-Maker
WILLIAM COLE

Just Me
MARIE HALL ETS

Happy Birthday, Sam
PAT HUTCHINS

Titch
PAT HUTCHINS

Sara and the Door
VIRGINIA JENSEN

Leo the Late Bloomer
ROBERT KRAUS

Eyes, Nose, Fingers, Toes
RUTH KRAUSS

I Can Do It by Myself
LESSIE J. LITTLE

If I Were a Mother
KAZUE MIZUMURA

*This Little Pig Went to Market:
Play Rhymes*
MOTHER GOOSE

How Do I Put It On?
SHIGEO WATANABE

Betsy and the Vacuum Cleaner
GUNILLA WOLDE

Rhythms, Rhymes, and Fingerplays

I Have a Nose

On my face I have a nose, (point to nose)
And way down here I have ten toes. (point to toes)
I have two eyes that I can blink. (blink eyes)
I have a head to help me think. (hands on head)
I have a chin and very near, (point to chin)
I have two ears to help me hear. (hands one ears)
I have a mouth with which to speak, (point to mouth)
And when I run I use my feet. (tap feet on floor)
Here are arms to hold up high, (arms held high)
And here's a hand to wave good-bye. (wave)

We Can Jump (follow the actions)

We can jump, jump, jump.
We can hop, hop, hop.
We can clap, clap, clap.

We can stop, stop, stop.
We can nod our heads for "yes,"
We can shake our heads for "no."
We can bend our knees a little bit
And sit . . . down . . . slow.

Follow-up Ideas

Toddlers need lots of experience with words and language. The more you talk to them, the better their language will develop. Talking through daily routines is sharing through language and helps make the routines more interesting.

At bath time, touch and name each part of the body as you help your child wash. ("I scrub one knee. What am I scrubbing?" "My knee!")

When dressing, children like to repeat the names of everything they put on them and why the item is useful. ("My hat is on my head to keep it warm.")

At nap time, talk about what you did this morning and what you will do together *after* the nap. ("When you wake up we'll go for a walk.")

Craft

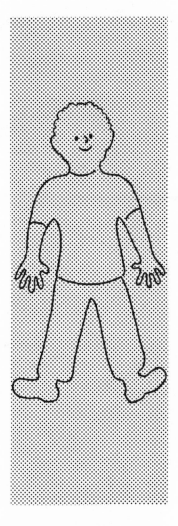

A Me Picture

You will need: a large grocery sack or wide shelf paper

a pencil

scissors

crayons or markers

Cut the bottom from the sack and cut up one side so it will lie flat. Have your child lay down on the sack and quickly trace around him or her. Draw on the features and talk about parts of the body and the clothes that cover them. Color the Me picture and hang it on a door or the refrigerator, or send it as a special card to a grandparent or friend. When you make this activity part of a birthday celebration, you can compare it with last year's Me picture.

A change of clothes could be made from newspaper or another paper sack and paper-clipped or taped to the Me picture as situations or weather changes.

Program Notes

Opening Routine

Sign   "Me"—Point to self with index finger.

ST   Book: *I Can Do It by Myself.* Have children pretend to do the things along with the story.

A   "I Have a Nose" fingerplay

ST   Book: *My Hands Can*

A   "We Can Jump" action rhyme

ST   Book: *My Feet Do*

A   Hand and feet actions (clapping, waving, jumping, dancing, tiptoeing)

QT   Parent and child look at book together and trace child's hands on piece of paper. Hand out typing paper and pencils for parents to trace their children's hands on the paper. Label with child's name.

G   Outline of hands (above)

Closing Routine   Exit storyspace with feet doing something different (dancing, skipping, tiptoeing).

Notes

Monkeys

Stories Shared

I'm a Monkey
ROBERT KRAUS

Other Stories of Interest

Little Gorilla
RUTH BORNSTEIN

The Monkey and the Crocodile
PAUL GALDONE

Jacko
JOHN GOODALL

Five Little Monkey Business
JULIET KEPES

Run, Little Monkeys!
Run, Run, Run!
JULIET KEPES

Wise Monkey Tale
BETSY MAESTRO

Monkey See, Monkey Do
HELEN OXENBURY

Animals 'Round the Mulberry Bush
TONY PALAZZO

Caps for Sale
ESPHYR SLOBODKINA

Monkeys and the Pedlar
SUZANNE SUBA

Rhythms, Rhymes, and Fingerplays

Five Little Monkeys

Five little monkeys (hold up five fingers)
Swinging in a tree. (swing hands over head)
Teasing Mr. Crocodile (shake one finger)
"You can't catch me. (point to self, shake head)
You can't catch me!"
Up comes Mr. Crocodile quiet as can be.
(palms together, move hands upward)
Snap! (clap hands, sharply)

[Repeat with "Four," Three," "Two," and "One" little monkeys]

Pop Goes the Weasel

All around the mulberry bush (turn in circle)
The monkey chased the weasel (make grabbing motions)
The monkey thought 'twas all in fun. (shape one finger)
Pop! (clap hands) goes the weasel.

Monkey See, Monkey Do

When you clap, clap, clap your hands (clap hands)
The monkey clap, clap, claps his hands. (clap hands)
Monkey see (shade eyes with hands)
Monkey do (repeat first motion)
Monkey does the same as you. (point to child)

[Repeat with "stamp, stamp, stamp your feet..."
"jump, jump, jump up high..."
"make, make, make a funny face..."
"turn, turn, turn around..."]

Follow-up Ideas

Monkey see, monkey do: This simple version of "Simple Simon" teaches your child to listen and follow directions. Begin with small actions ("touch your nose"; "reach up high"; "clap your hands") and save bigger actions for out-of-doors or places with lots of room ("run fast"; "jump high"; "twirl around").

Water painting: Inexpensive painting books are available at department stores with the colors imbedded into the pages. When you add water with a paintbrush, the colors come out. These books will not promote artistic ability in your child, but they are good for learning to work with a small tool like a paintbrush.

Another way to paint with water in warm weather is to fill a can with water and let your child "paint" the house, the sidewalk or driveway. Talk about evaporation as the water dries and becomes invisible.

Craft

Clown-Shape Puzzle

You will need: brightly colored pieces of felt in the following shapes: 1 rectangle; 1 triangle; 1 large and 1 small circle; 2 small stars; 1 crescent (for smile)

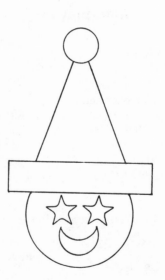

For circles, trace around objects (margarine tubs or salt shakers) onto the felt. Use a ruler to draw rectangle and triangle. Do not worry about pencil marks since the pieces can easily be flipped over when used. Draw stars and crescent freehand.

Talk with your child about the shapes of these puzzle pieces and their colors. Take turns arranging and rearranging them on a table, sofa cushion, or flannelboard to form a clown's face. Make additional pieces and see what kinds of designs or pictures you can create.

Program Notes

Opening
Routine

Sign "Monkey"—Hands curled under arms; scratching motion along sides of body.

ST Book: *I'm a Monkey*

A "Monkey See, Monkey Do" action rhyme. Have a puppet be the leader with children following his actions.

A "Five Little Monkeys" fingerplay

ST Glove puppet of "Five Little Monkeys." After monkeys are all taken from the tree by the crocodile, have the crocodile put them back again as you count them. This reassurance that the monkeys are all right is needed by some toddlers.

A "Pop Goes the Weasel" action rhyme

QT Participants look at books together.

G Paper sack monkeys

Needed: Lunch-sized paper sacks; monkey face (photocopied); 12" yarn; glue

Cut out face and glue it to the lunch sack as shown. Glue yarn to other side of sack for tail. Children can wear the monkey puppet on their hands or when he stands on his head, he can hold treasures.

Closing
Routine

--- Notes ---

Parades

Stories Shared

Parade
DONALD CREWS

Drummer Hoff
ED EMBERLEY

More Stories to Share at Home

Look What I Can Do
JOSE ARUEGO

Hurrah for Freddie
ROBERT BRIGHT

*Little Bear Marches in the
St. Patrick's Day Parade*
JANICE BRUSTLEIN

St. Patrick's Day in the Morning
EVE BUNTING

Parade Book
ED EMBERLEY

In the Forest
MARIE HALL ETS

Wait for William
MARJORIE FLACK

Follow Me, the Leader
DOROTHEA FOX

One Dancing Drum
GAIL KREDENSER

Nursery Rhymes

*Pezzo the Peddler and the Circus
Elephant*
ESPHYR SLOBODKINA

Crash! Bang! Boom!
PETER SPIER

Counting Carnival
FEENIE ZINER

Rhythms, Rhymes, and Fingerplays

The Finger Band

The finger band is coming to town,
Coming to town, coming to town.
The finger band is coming to town,
So early in the morning.
(wiggling fingers, move hands from behind back to front)
This is the way they wear their hats,
Wear their hats, wear their hats.
This is the way they wear their hats,
So early in the morning.
(hands form pointed hats on heads)

[Repeat with "This is the way they wave their flags..."
(hands above head, wave back and forth)
"This is the way they beat their drums..."
(beating motion with hands)
"This is the way they blow their horns..."
(hands cup mouth like horn)

"This is the way they clash their cymbals . . ."
(clap hands together)
"This is the way they march along . . ."
(stand tall, march lifting feet high)]

The finger band is going away,
Going away, going away.
The finger band is going away,
So early in the morning
(wiggling fingers, move hands from front to behind back)

Follow-up Ideas

Play "Follow-the-Leader," which teaches how to be observant and copy another's movements, and how to lead.

Place-in-line game: Play with three blocks, toys, or any objects. Have your child make a line of the items. Now tell what is "first," "middle," "last." Also good for learning to follow directions: "Put the block in front of the truck; behind the truck; and so forth."

Craft

Homemade Musical Instruments

Drums: Empty oatmeal boxes, metal pans, or wooden bowls. Beat with hands or wooden spoons.

Horns: Cardboard tubes with holes poked in sides will produce different notes. Hum or sing through one end to create music.

Tamborine: A ring of keys or metal measuring spoons. Shake away from the body. Also, tie bells on a small aluminum pie tin for a good effect.

Cymbals: Two metal lids or aluminum pie pans. Bang together.

Shaker: A small container with a tightly fitting lid that is half-filled with beans or macaroni. Shake fast or slow.

Rhythm Sticks: Two wooden spoons. Bang together.

Homemade musical instruments are a lot of fun. Many things in the home can be turned into music makers. Use them to create a parade around the house, to accompany television programs, or while listening to the radio or a record.

Program Notes

**Opening
Routine**

Sign "Drum"—Make motions like playing a drum.

P Puppet brings out drum (oatmeal container) and shows how to beat it, then distributes paper plates to children to be used as drums. They put plates on floor and beat on them, following the puppet's lead: fast, slow, and so forth. Puppet then introduces the upcoming story.

ST Book: *Drummer Hoff.* Make "pa-rum-pum-pum" noises during transitions in the story. Children may beat their drums, too.

A Stretch.

ST Book: *Parade*

A "The Finger Band" action rhyme

CD March around the storyspace as the finger band: wearing hats, waving hands and flags, playing horns, drums, and cymbals. March back to starting point (parent's lap).

QT Parent and child look at books together.

G Parade flag

Needed: paper triangle; plastic straws; marker; tape

Cut or punch two holes on one end of the paper. Print the child's name on both sides. Insert the straw as shown and tape the back to keep flag from slipping.

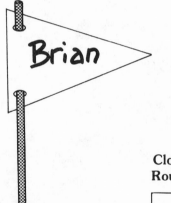

**Closing
Routine** Parade out of storyspace waving flags.

───── **Notes** ─────

Peek, Peek . . . Hide and Seek

Stories Shared

Spot's First Walk
ERIC HILL

The Box with Red Wheels
MAUD PETERSHAM AND
MISKA PETERSHAM

More Stories to Share at Home

Each Peach Pear Plum
ALLAN AHLBERG

Calico Cat Looks Around
DONALD CHARLES

You Go Away
DOROTHY COREY

What's Inside?
DUANNE DAUGHTRY

The Hunter and the Animals
TOMIE dePAOLA

Boxes! Boxes!
LEONARD EVERETT FISHER

Holes and Peeks
ANN JONES

What's Inside the Box?
ETHEL KESSLER

Mother Goose: 77 Verses

Who's There? Open the Door
BRUNO MUNARI

I Spy
LUCILLE OGLE

It Looked like Spilt Milk
CHARLES SHAW

Things We See
ANTHONY THOMAS

Rhythms, Rhymes, and Fingerplays

Where Are the Baby Mice?

Where are the baby mice (make a fist)
"Squeak, squeak, squeak!"
I cannot see them (peer into fist)
Peek! Peek! Peek!
Here they come out from their hole in the wall
1, 2, 3, 4, 5 . . . (extend fingers as counted)
And, that's all! (turn palm up, hand extended)

Indians Are Creeping

The Indians are creeping (two fingers tiptoe up forearm)
Shhhhhhhhh! (raise index finger to lips)
The Indians are creeping (repeat above)
Shhhhhh!
They do not make a sound (fingers tiptoe up arm)
As their feet touch the ground.
The Indians are creeping (repeat above)
Shhhhhhhh!

The Window

> See the window I have here
> (form "window" with thumbs and index fingers)
> So big and high and square.
> I can stand in front of it
> (peer through fingers)
> And see the things out there.
> I . . . see . . . You! (point)

Follow-up Ideas

Window watching: Look out of a window and ask, "What do you see?" Is it sunny, rainy, snowy? Are there birds, squirrels, or people? Can you see trucks, bicycles, cars?

Do the same thing at night, looking for dark places, lights (moving or blinking?), the moon or stars. This activity helps toddlers to be observant and increases their vocabulary.

Play "Hide-and-Seek": Save plastic hosiery "eggs" for a hide-and-seek game. Put small toys or treats inside the eggs and hide them (not too well) throughout the house. Give hints to your child like, "There's one hiding in the kitchen near the table," or "Look by the lamp where Daddy likes to sit." This game is fun and helps your child learn to follow directions. When all the eggs are found, have a party and open the eggs to discover the prizes inside.

Craft

Touchbox

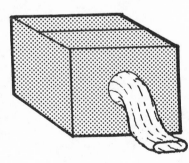

You will need: cardboard box with flaps or lid that closes it completely

an old sock

glue

scissors or box cutter

straight pins

contact paper or paint

Cut a hole in one side of the box (not the side that is open). The hole must be large enough to insert your hand. Cover the box with contact paper or paint.

Cut the ribbed edge (top) off the sock and glue one end around the hole on the *inside* of the box. Pin with straight pins to hold sock in place until glue dries thoroughly, then remove the pins.

Put an object in the box and close the lid. As the children reach through the sock, they feel the object. Ask the children to name the object or describe what it feels like, rather than trying to pull it out of the hole. Ask questions: "Is it soft or hard? little or big? warm or cold?" and so on. This activity is good for language development.

Open the lid and take out the object, naming it, and describing the way it looks or feels. Children learn to discriminate between objects by the way they feel and look based on descriptions learned from others. Put the same object back in the box or use a different object. Also let the children put something in the box for you to feel.

Program Notes

Opening Routine   Play "Peek-a-Boo" a couple of times to introduce the theme.

ST   Display book: *Box with Red Wheels* (flannelboard story)

A   "Where Are the Baby Mice?" fingerplay

ST   Book: *Spot's First Walk*

A   "The Window" fingerplay

Sign   "Surprise"—Place right hand at your temple and sharply open fingers wide. Open eyes wide in surprise at same time.

ST   Touchbox has puppet inside. Each child reaches into box to feel what's inside, then peeks into the top of the box to see if they guessed right.

P   Puppet leads children in the fingerplay, "Indians Are Creeping."

QT   Participants look at books together.

G   Turn-around faces

   Needed: Two 3-oz. white plastic cups; brass fastener; scissors; marker

   Cut a 1″ hole in the side of one cup. With a marker, draw faces (happy, sad, silly, scared) on the four sides of the second cup. Slide the second cup inside the first and attach the two with a brass fastener through the cup bottoms. The inside cup will spin displaying different faces through the hole as it turns.

Closing Routine

--- Notes ---

Rabbits

Stories Shared

The Rabbit
JOHN BURNINGHAM

Where Is It?
TANA HOBAN

Morning, Rabbit, Morning
MARY CALDWELL

More Stories to Share at Home

Humbug Rabbit
LORNA BALIAN

Golden Egg Book
MARGARET WISE BROWN

Rabbit for Easter
CAROL CARRICK

Let's Make Rabbits
LEO LIONNI

Mother Goose

I Am a Bunny
OLE RISOM

Max's New Suit
ROSEMARY WELLS

All the Little Bunnies
ELIZABETH BRIDGMAN

Miffy's Dream
DICK BRUNA

Baby Bunny for You
WALTER CHANDOHA

No, No Natalie
GRACE E. MOREMAN

Marshmallow
CLARE TURLAY NEWBERRY

My Bunny Feels Soft
CHARLOTTE STEINER

Mr. Rabbit and the Lovely Present
CHARLOTTE ZOLOTOW

Rhythms, Rhymes, and Fingerplays

Little Rabbit

I saw a little rabbit go hop, hop, hop.
(hop in place)
I saw his long ears go flop, flop, flop.
(hands above head, "flop" wrists over and back)
I saw his little eyes go wink, wink, wink.
(blink eyes)
I saw his little nose go twink, twink, twink.
(wiggle nose)
I said, "Little Rabbit, won't you stay?"
(make beckoning motion)
He looked at me and . . . hopped away!
(hop quickly)

Here Is a Bunny

Here is a bunny with ears so funny.
(hands above head to make ears, flop wrists)
Here is his hole in the ground.
(arms create circle in front of body)
When a noise he hears,
(clap hands sharply)
He pricks up his ears
(hands above head, held straight up)
And jumps in his hole in the ground.
(jump into a crouching position)

Follow-up Ideas

Animal riddles are good for times when you are waiting for things to happen (such as being called into the doctor's office). Try these:

I eat grass.	I gallop.	I have feathers.
I say moo.	I trot.	I peck and peck.
What am I?	My hooves go	I say cluck, cluck.
	clip, clop.	What am I?
	What am I?	

Visit the zoo or a pet shop. Go at feeding time. Find out what different animals and birds eat. Find out how they eat.

Do they have claws? Teeth? Beaks? Feathers? Fur? Fins?

Craft

Rabbit Cup Puppet

You will need: a paper cup

a straw

tape

a picture of a rabbit small enough to fit in the cup (draw one or cut from magazine or greeting card)

Poke a hole in the bottom of the cup large enough so that a straw can easily slide through. Tape the rabbit picture to one end of the straw and slide the other end of the straw down through the hole in the bottom of the cup. Operate the puppet by sliding the straw up and down. While reciting the rhyme "Here Is a Bunny" (above), let your child operate the rabbit puppet, making it appear and disappear at the proper times.

RABBIT HOLE

Program Notes

Opening Routine	Introduce theme with toy rabbit, rabbit puppet, or regular storytime puppet wearing paper rabbit ears.
Sign	"Rabbit"—Cross hands at wrists with index and middle fingers extended (like rabbits). Quickly bend extended fingers twice.
ST	Book: *Morning, Rabbit, Morning*
A	"Little Rabbit" fingerplay
ST	Display book: *The Rabbit* (flannelboard story)
A	"Here Is a Bunny" fingerplay
ST	Book: *Where Is It?*
P	Puppet wearing paper-plate rabbit ears distributes the same kind of ears to each child with instructions to put them on.
CD	Pretending to be bunnies, children hop (high, low, fast, slow), crouch low to hide, and hop home (to parent).
QT	Little bunnies share a book with their parent.
G	Paper-plate ears

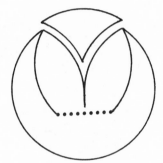

Needed: Paper plate; scissors; stapler; string or ribbon

Cut a curved quarter section from the paper plate (as shown). Make two curved cuts opposite the first creating two "ears." Fold ears forward along line between second cuts.

Staple the ends of the plate together to form the cap and attach string or ribbon to be tied under child's chin.

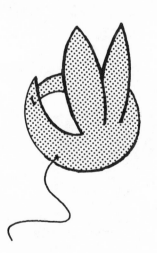

Closing Routine	All rabbits hop out of the storyspace together.

Notes

Rain

Stories Shared

Rainbow of My Own
DON FREEMAN

Mushroom in the Rain
MIRRA GINSBURG

More Stories to Share at Home

My Red Umbrella
ROBERT BRIGHT

Caught in the Rain
BEATRIZ FERRO

Umbrella
JUN IWAMATSU

Letter to Amy
EZRA JACK KEATS

When It Rains
MARY DEBALL KWITZ

One Misty Moisty Morning
MOTHER GOOSE

Rain Drop Splash
ALVIN TRESSELT

Mr. Gumpy's Motor Car
JOHN BURNINGHAM

Dandelion
DON FREEMAN

Rain
ROBERT KALAN

James and the Rain
KARLA KUSKIN

The Little Girl and the Rain
MILENA LUKESOVA

Peter Spier's Rain
PETER SPIER

Rhythms, Rhymes, and Fingerplays

Rain

Rain on the green grass,
(wave hands low)
Rain on the tree.
(wave hands high)
Rain on the housetop,
(hands form point over head like roof)
But not on me!
(point to self)

Eency Weency Spider

Eency-weency spider went up the water spout.
(wiggle fingers upward in front of body)
Down came the rain and washed the spider out.
(sweep arms down and to one side)
Out came the sun and dried up all the rain,
(arms form circle over head)
And the eency-weency spider went up the spout again.
(wiggle fingers upward again)

Busy Windshield Wipers

(hold arms up in front of body and move them from side to side)
Busy windshield wipers go
A-dash, a-dash, a-dash.
Wiping all the drops away
Splash, splash, splash.

Follow-up Ideas

Playing in water is educational for toddlers. Stay close by and play with your child until safety rules are learned (stay away from hot water; don't throw water; keep objects out of the mouth). The kitchen sink, bathtub, or wading pool are good places for waterplay. When clean-up time comes, toddlers can be good helpers.

Good water toys are sponges, plastic containers (some with holes), measuring cups, eye droppers, funnels, jar lids, or anything unbreakable. Add interest with a squirt of shaving cream or some bubble bath.

This is a great language-building time. "Pour, spill, sprinkle, splash, spurt, squirt, dribble, flow, flood, trickle, and spray" all describe different ways that water behaves. Each word sounds like what it describes. Use these words to increase your child's vocabulary and the way he thinks about water.

Pry the ball off an empty roll-on deodorant jar and wash the bottle out. Fill it with tempera paint and push the ball back on. Presto: a giant ball-point pen that paints. Cover a table with newspaper and let your child create pictures on shelf paper or paper sacks.

Craft

A Rainbow

You will need: a paper plate

colored paper streamers

scissors

a popsicle stick

tape or a stapler

a marker

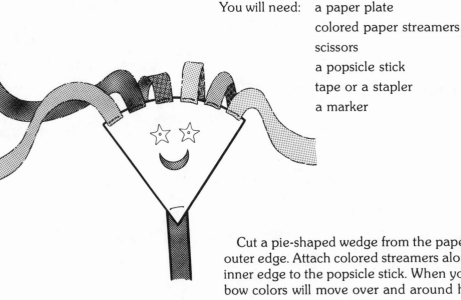

Cut a pie-shaped wedge from the paper plate and draw a face near the outer edge. Attach colored streamers along the outer edge, and staple the inner edge to the popsicle stick. When your child holds the stick, the rainbow colors will move over and around him or her like a rainbow!

Program Notes

**Opening
Routine**

Sign "Rain"—Place hands at shoulder level, palms facing out, fingers curved. Bend hands at wrist twice (indicating rain falling).

ST Display book: *Mushroom in the Rain.* Using a real umbrella and stuffed animals or puppets, tell the story and open the umbrella a little at a time. Afterward let each child come and sit under the umbrella.

A "Busy Windshield Wipers" fingerplay

ST Book: *Rainbow of My Own*

A "Rain" fingerplay

ST "Eency Weency Spider" (flannelboard rhyme)

A "Eency Weency Spider" action rhyme. Stand and stretch high and low during the rhyme. Do the rhyme twice; once loudly with big actions and again with smaller actions and quiet voices.

QT Parent and child look at books together.

G Rainbows of their own (see above for directions)

**Closing
Routine** Exit storyspace with rainbows flying high above heads.

Rainbows created by participants

— Notes —

Sizes

Stories Shared

Blue Sea
ROBERT KALAN

Sizes
JAN PIENKOWSKI

More Stories to Share at Home

I'm Too Small, You're Too Big
JUDI BARRETT

Big Puppy and Little Puppy
IRMA SIMONTON BLACK

Little Gorilla
RUTH BORNSTEIN

A Dinosaur Is Too Big
ELIZABETH BRAM

Lion and the Rat
JEAN DE LA FONTAINE

The Mouse and the Elephant
JOAN HEWETT

Big Ones, Little Ones
TANA HOBAN

You'll Soon Grow into Them, Titch
PAT HUTCHINS

Mother Goose Nursery Rhymes

The Three Bears

Great Big Enormous Turnip
ALEKSEI TOLSTOY

Rhythms, Rhymes, and Fingerplays

Where Is Thumbkin?

Where is Thumbkin? (hands behind back)
Where is Thumbkin?
Here I am! (right thumb extended in front)
Here I am! (left thumb extended)
How are you this morning? (wiggle right thumb)
Very well, I thank you. (wiggle left thumb)
Run and play. (right hand behind back)
Run and play. (left hand behind back)

[Repeat above using "Pointer" (index finger)
   "Tall-man" (middle finger)
   "Ring-man" (ring finger)
   "Baby" (little finger)
   "Everyone" (all fingers)]

Sometimes I Am Tall

Sometimes I am tall. (stretch up on toes)
Sometimes I am small. (crouch down low)
Sometimes I am very, very tall. (stretch and reach up hands)
Sometimes I am very, very small. (crouch low to floor)
Sometimes tall . . . (stretch up)
Sometimes small . . . (crouch low)
See how I am now. (stand normally)

Follow-up Ideas

When on a trip to the grocery store, look for fruits and vegetables that are: small and round, big and round, long and thin, unusual in shape, rough or smooth to the touch.

Use pictures in magazines to teach words relating to size. See if you can find: short or tall people, fat or skinny dogs, big or little cars, and so on.

Go on a rock-collecting walk. Talk about the sizes of rocks as you pick them up and sort them. Place in an egg carton when you get home.

Craft

Flannelboard

You will need: a piece of flat, heavy cardboard

a piece of flannel or felt, 1″ larger than the dimensions of the cardboard piece

scrap pieces of materials with naps (felt, flannel, velvet, corduroy) or sandpaper

glue

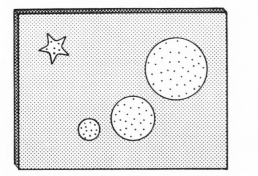 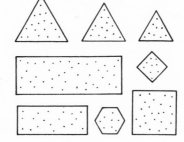

Wipe the cardboard with a clean cloth to remove dust. Spread glue over all the surface on one side of the cardboard. Put the flannel over the glue and smooth flat. Let dry thoroughly. Overlap edges of flannel over cardboard and glue to the other side. Weight or pin edges so they will dry flat. Let dry thoroughly.

Cut out shapes from the material scraps. Make basic shapes (circles, triangles, and so forth), animal shapes, people shapes, or crazy shapes. Use pictures from magazines or coloring books for patterns or glue these pictures to the material for ready-made flannel pieces. Vary the shapes in size: small, medium, and large. Pictures glued onto the smooth side of sandpaper will also stick to a flannelboard (and cutting sandpaper sharpens scissors!).

Show your child how the pieces will stick to the flannelboard; then let the child play with them alone or arrange the pieces together to tell a story, make a picture, or teach about sizes.

Program Notes

**Opening
Routine**

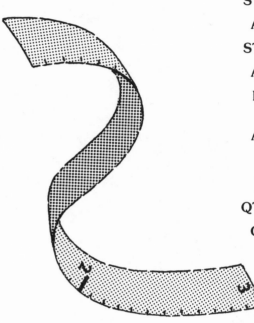

Sign   "Little"—Extend index fingers, and move them toward each other. "Big"—Open hands, with palms facing each other. Move hands away from each other.

ST   Book: *Sizes*

A   "Where Is Thumbkin" fingerplay

ST   Display book: *Blue Sea* (flannelboard story)

A   "Sometimes I Am Tall" action rhyme

P   Have puppet appear with yardstick, and measure children to see if they are bigger than the puppet.

A   Puppet brings out nesting cans or nesting dolls (a series of items that fit inside each other). Let each child help as the cans are taken apart (big, small, smaller) and put together again (little, big, bigger). Return cans to touchbox when finished.

QT   Parent and child look at books together.

G   Measuring strip

Needed: 36″ strip of material or paper; marker

Mark on strip 1-foot, 2-feet, 3-feet, and beyond 3 feet. Strip can be attached to child's bedroom door or refrigerator to measure height.

**Closing
Routine**

--- Notes ---

Sounds

Stories Shared

Moo, Baa, La, La, La
SANDRA BOYNTON

What Do the Animals Say?
GRACE SKAAR

Goodnight Owl
PAT HUTCHINS

More Stories to Share at Home

Pigs Say Oink
MARTHA G. ALEXANDER

Fee Fi Fo Fum
RAYMOND BRIGGS

SHHhhh . . . Bang!
A Whispering Book
MARGARET WISE BROWN

What's That Noise?
LOIS KAUFFMAN

Roar and More
KARLA KUSKIN

Old MacDonald Had a Farm

Who Said, "Meow?"
MARIA POLUSHKIN

Buzz, Buzz, Buzz
BYRON BARTON

Indoor Noisy Book
MARGARET WISE BROWN

Hullabaloo A B C
BEVERLY CLEARY

All Sizes of Noises
KARLA KUSKIN

I Hear
LUCILLE OGLE

Morning
MARIA POLUSHKIN

Gobble! Growl! Grunt!
PETER SPIER

Rhythms, Rhymes, and Fingerplays

Boom! Bang!

Boom, bang, boom, bang!
(beat one fist in other palm)
Rumpety, lumpety, bump!
(slap hands on knees)
Zoom, zam, zoom, zam!
(shoot hands across front of body)
Clippety, clappety, clump!
(nod head from side to side)
Rustles and bustles
(hug hands to shoulders)
And swishes and zings,
(lean side to side)
What wonderful noises
(throw hands over head)
A thunderstorm brings!!
(clap hands together)

Pound Goes the Hammer

Pound, pound, pound-pound-pound
(pound one fist into other palm)
Goes the hammer.
Pound-pound-pound.

Bzz, bzz, bzz-bzz-bzz,
(hand open, thumb up, make sawing motion)
Goes the saw.
Bzz-bzz-bzz.
Chop, chop, chop-chop-chop,
(hand open, chop into other palm)
Goes the axe.
Chop-chop-chop.

Follow-up Ideas

Talk about:

1. Close your eyes and listen. What sounds do you hear? Cars? Horns? Running water? Radio or television? What else?
2. Put your fingers on your throat when singing or talking. Do you feel your throat tingle?
3. While talking, gently pat your chest or your mouth to make the sound change. Can you do that while singing?
4. Put different-sized items in small covered containers and shake. Does macaroni sound different from raisins? cereal?
5. Practice talking in a loud voice . . . now a normal voice . . . now a whisper. Can you be perfectly still? Can you hear other sounds when you are still?

Craft

Paper Plate Banjo

You will need: two paper plates

scissors

a paint stirrer

glue

four rubber bands

Cut a hole in the middle of one plate. Glue the rims of the plates together with the insides facing. Let dry. Glue the paint stirrer to the plate with the hole (but not covering the hole). After the glue dries, stretch the rubber bands, two on each side of the stirrer, over the hole in the plate. Tape rubber bands to prevent their sliding off plate. Strum gently to make music!

Program Notes

Opening Routine Introduce theme with different sounds: a whistle, a toy piano, paper crumpling, hands clapping, and so forth. It's best if you can keep the source hidden to give children a chance to guess what the sound is. Always name the source and the kind of sound (loud, soft, shrill).

Sign "Listen"—Cup right hand to ear as if trying to hear.

ST Book: *Moo, Baa, La, La, La*

A "Pound Goes the Hammer" action rhyme

ST Book: *What Do the Animals Say?* Have children help make the sounds throughout the story.

A "Boom! Bang!" action rhyme

ST Display book: *Goodnight Owl* (flannelboard story using only 5 different birds)

A Stretching

QT Parent and child look at books together.

G Tamborines

Needed: Small aluminum pie tins (pot pie size); paper punch; yarn; small bells

Punch three holes evenly spaced around the edge of the pie tin.

With the yarn, securely tie a bell in each hole. Shake the pie tin and the bells will jingle.

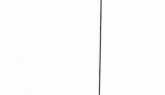

Closing Routine

─── Notes ───

Trains

Stories Shared

1, 2, 3 to the Zoo
ERIC CARLE

Freight Train
DONALD CREWS

More Stories to Share at Home

Whistle for the Train
MARGARET WISE BROWN

Choo Choo
VIRGINIA LEE BURTON

Everyday Train
AMY EHRLICH

All Aboard the Train
ETHEL KESSLER AND
LEONARD KESSLER

Little Train
LOIS LENSKI

One Is the Engine
ESTHER MEEKS

Mother Goose

Little Engine That Could
WATTY PIPER

Railroad A B C
JACK TOWEND

Little Red Train
GUY WEELEN

Puff
WILLIAM WONDRISKA

I Like Trains
CATHERINE WOOLLEY

If I Drove a Train
MIRIAM YOUNG

Rhythms, Rhymes, and Fingerplays

Here Is the Engine

(count train cars on fingers or toes as you say the rhyme)
Here is the engine on the track. (thumb)
Here is the coal car, just in back. (pointer)
Here is the boxcar to carry the freight. (middle finger)
Here is the mail car. Don't be late! (ring finger)
Way back here at the end of the train
Rides the caboose through the sun and the rain. (wiggle pinky)

Here Comes the Choo-Choo Train

Here comes the choo-choo train
(elbows against sides, arms make forward circles)
Puffing down the track.
Now it's going forward . . .
Now it's going back.
(reverse circles)
Hear the bell a-ringing.
(one hand above head, make bell-ringing motion)

Ding . . . Ding . . . Ding . . . Ding
Hear the whistle blow.
(cup hands around mouth)
Whooooo-Whoooooo!
Chug, chug, chug, chug
(make side circles slowly, then pick up speed)
ch . . . ch . . . ch . . . ch . . . ch . . . ch . . . ch . . .
Shhhhhh . . .
(fold hands in lap)
Everywhere it goes.

Follow-up Ideas

Sounds fascinate small children and they love to imitate them. Make up a song or play a guessing game involving sounds of living things (cats, dogs, cows) and of familiar non-living things (cars, trains, clocks, whistles).

Tie several small boxes together with shoestrings or twine to make a pull train for your child. Shoe boxes (with the lids left off) are perfect for small toys or stuffed animals can ride in them. Talk about the train cars and where they come in line: first, middle, last.

Craft

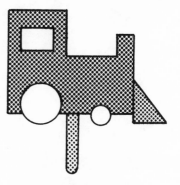

Train Stick Puppets

You will need: construction paper, cut in 3″×5″ rectangles
black construction paper (for engine and wheels)
scissors
crayons or markers
glue and tape
popsicle sticks

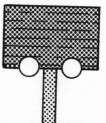

Make various train cars in the follow manner:

Engine: 3″×5″ black construction paper
1″ square black paper (smoke stack)
2″ square black paper, with window (cab)
triangle of black paper (scoop)
2 wheels
1 popsicle stick

Train cars: 3″×5″ construction paper (various colors for each car)
2 wheels for each car
1 popsicle stick
(Decorate the train cars with doors, slats, and windows.)

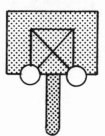

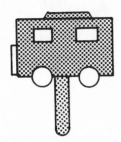

Caboose: 3"×5" red construction paper

2 wheels

1" square cut in half (observation deck and back railing)

1 popsicle stick

Attach pieces of each train car with glue, and tape the car to a popsicle stick. Stand the train up along the back of a sofa with the sticks between the cushions or have a train parade when friends visit. This is also a good opportunity to talk about colors, shapes, first-middle-last, and other kinds of vehicles with your child.

Program Notes

Opening Routine

Sign   "Train"—With only the index and middle fingers extended, slide the right fingers lightly up and down the backs of the left fingers.

ST   Book: *1, 2, 3 to the Zoo*

A   "Here Comes the Choo-Choo Train" action rhyme

ST   Book: *Freight Train*. Reinforce with flannelboard figures of the train cars. Be certain to remove all of figures from flannelboard before proceeding.

P   Puppet appears with train stick puppets (see above) looking for someone to help play train. Distribute one stick puppet to each child, keeping the engine for the puppet. Children line up behind the storyteller and "chug" around the room (go fast, slow, straight or winding; have them make train noises and wave at their parent as they pass). Park the train back in the touchbox when finished.

ST   "Here Is the Engine" rhyme using the flannelboard train cars

A   "Here Is the Engine" fingerplay

QT   Parent and child look at books together.

G   Train bookmark. Photocopy and distribute: "Here Comes the Train."

Closing Routine   Exit storyspace chugging like a train.

┌─ Notes ───┐
│   │
│   │
│   │
│   │
│   │
│   │
│   │
└──┘

Vehicles

Stories Shared

Airport
BYRON BARTON

School Bus
DONALD CREWS

Mr. Gumpy's Outing
JOHN BURNINGHAM

More Stories to Share at Home

A B C of Cars and Trucks
ANN ALEXANDER

Bears on Wheels
STAN BERENSTAIN AND
JAN BERENSTAIN

Truck
DONALD CREWS

Dig, Drill, Dump, Fill
TANA HOBAN

*A B C of Cars, Trucks
and Machines*
ADELAIDE HOLL

Behind the Wheel
EDWARD KOREN

If I Flew a Plane
MIRIAM YOUNG

Wheels
BYRON BARTON

Shawn's Red Bike
PETRONELLA BREINBURG

Favorite Best Mother Goose Rhymes

How Do I Go?
MARY ANN HOBERMAN

Big Red Bus
ETHEL KESSLER

Hop Aboard! Here We Go!
RICHARD SCARRY

*Giant Nursery Book of Things
That Go*
GEORGE J. ZAFFO

Rhythms, Rhymes, and Fingerplays

Auto, Auto

Auto, auto, may I have a ride? (point to self)
Yes, sir; yes, sir. Step inside. (nod head, motion toward you)
Pour in the water, (pouring motion with right hand)
Pump in the gas. (pouring motion with left hand)
Chug-away, chug-away, but not too fast! (steering motion)

If I Were . . .

If I were an airplane (spread arms wide like wings)
I would fly up in the sky (arms still out, lean left and right)
If I were a tricycle (pump legs as if peddling)
I would wave as I went by. (wave)
If I were a dump truck (elbow bent, hand on shoulder)
I would dump my heavy load. (let hand fall)
But if I were a car or bus
I'd roll on down the road. (roll hands over each other)
If I were a choo-choo train (hands close to sides)
Along the tracks I'd chug. (push-pull alternately with arms)
And if I were a steam shovel (hands near knees, palms up)
I would have a big hole dug. (scooping motion with hands)
If I were a whirlybird (whirl hands over head)
I'd sing a whirly tune. (make whirrrring noise)
But if I were a rocket ship (palms together close to chest)
I'd Blast Off to the moon! (shoot hands upward)

Follow-up Ideas

When traveling with a toddler, take along a busy box. Fill a shoe box with household objects that your child can play with alone: covered containers with lids that snap on and off, a magnet and some large metal items, a piece of cardboard covered with aluminum foil to make a mirror, or a mesh bag from the produce department and some yarn (with tape around one end to make a point for weaving). Keep this busy box just for trips in the car to insure that it remains a special treat and will help pass the time for your toddler.

Craft

Pretend Steering Wheel

You will need: cardboard
an oatmeal box
a brass fastener
a clothes hanger cardboard tube (from pants hanger)
scissors
hole punch

Cut out a 9″ circle from cardboard and cut spaces in it to create a steering wheel. Punch a hole in the side of the oatmeal box near the top, and attach the steering wheel with the brass fastener.

Poke a hole to the right of the steering wheel and push the cardboard tube into it creating a gear shift lever. The tube should fit loose enough to be moved up and down. Place the cereal box between your child's knees, leaving hands free to "steer and change gears."

Program Notes

Opening Routine

Sign   "Car"—Make the motion of holding a steering wheel, move hands slightly up and down in opposition to each other (as if the wheel were moving).

ST   Book: *School Bus*

ST   Book: *Airport*

A   "If I Were..." action rhyme

ST   Display book: *Mr. Gumpy's Outing* (flannelboard story)

A   "Auto Auto" action rhyme

QT   Participants look at books together.

G   Paper-plate steering wheels

Needed: Paper plates; scissors

    Cut four triangular sections from the paper plate as shown to make a steering wheel. Hold the steering wheel in your hands and pretend to drive a car or bus.

Closing Routine   Exit storyspace pretending to drive different vehicles.

Notes

Wind

Stories Shared

The Wind Blew
PAT HUTCHINS

Who Took the Farmer's Hat?
JOAN L. NODSET

More Stories to Share at Home

In the Air
EUGENE BOOTH

When the Wind Blew
MARGARET WISE BROWN

Gilberto and the Wind
MARIE HALL ETS

North Wind and the Sun
JEAN DE LA FONTAINE

Up There: A Baby Bear Book
ERIC HILL

Little Mother Goose

I See the Winds
KAZUE MIZUMURA

Curious George Flies a Kite
MARGARET REY

March Wind
INEZ RICE

Great Big Air Book
RICHARD SCARRY

Follow the Wind
ALVIN TRESSELT

When the Wind Stops
CHARLOTTE ZOLOTOW

Rhythms, Rhymes, and Fingerplays

Wind Tricks

The wind is full of tricks today;
(shake index finger)
He blew my daddy's hat away.
(hand on head)
He chased our paper down the street
(reach down, to one side)
And almost blew us off our feet.
(jump up and down)
He makes the trees and bushes dance.
(wave arms)
Just listen to him howl and prance.
(cup hand to ear)
Whoooooooooo-oooooooooo.

Five Winds

(hold up fingers one at a time with each verse)
This little wind blows rain.
This little wind drifts snow.
This little wind whistles a tune. (whistle)
This little wind whispers low. (whisper)

And this little wind rocks baby birds
To and fro, to and fro, to and fro.
(hands together, rock back and forth)

Follow-up Ideas

Make a homemade fan by pleating a piece of paper. Secure the bottom with tape. Now you can make your own wind.

Observe the weather each day and talk about the changes. "Yesterday was sunny, but today it is raining." Mark on the calendar with crayons or stickers: sunny, rainy, snowy, cloudy, windy days.

To help your child understand that air is all around us, point out birds flying, put your hand close to a furnace vent, walk against the wind, blow bubbles, or drop confetti from your hand.

Craft

A Shape Kite

You will need: construction paper in bright colors

scissors

tape

string

a small stick or unsharpened pencil

Cut a circle, a triangle, a rectangle, a star, and a crescent shape from the construction paper, keeping them all about the same size. Lay the shapes in a line on a flat surface leaving one inch between them.

Tie one end of the string to the stick and lay the stick down in front of the line of shapes, leaving one inch between the stick and the first shape. Stretch the string across the shapes and tape it securely to the back of each one.

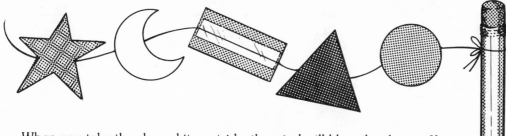

When you take the shape kite outside, the wind will blow the shapes. If there is no wind, hold the stick up high and walk or run with it. The shape kite will float above you like a banner.

By cutting shapes out of plastic margarine lids and painting them, you can create a wind indicator to attach outside. Punch holes on opposite edges of each shape and assemble in a line by tying them together with string. Attach to a tree or pole that is visible from a window, and your child can tell you if the wind is blowing outside without leaving the house.

Program Notes

Opening Routine

Sign   "Wind"—Fingers of both hands spread wide, palms facing about six inches apart. Move hands to the right and then to the left, as if blowing in the wind.

ST   Book: *Who Took the Farmer's Hat?* Use a real straw hat to display the different positions of the hat in the story and to demonstrate each animal's point of view.

A   "Wind Tricks" action rhyme

ST   Display book: *The Wind Blew* (flannelboard story)

A   "Five Winds" fingerplay

QT   Participants look at books together.

G   Pinwheels

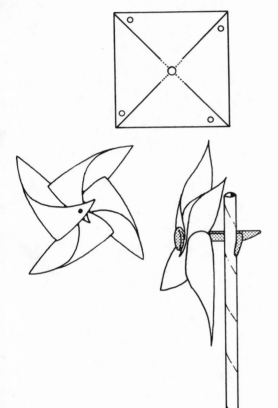

Needed: 4″ square of typing paper; plastic drinking straw; scissors; paper punch; brass fastener

Flatten one end of straw and punch a hole in it. Fold paper diagonally in both directions. Punch hole at center (while folded). Cut along folds to within 1″ of hole forming four petals. Punch a hole in the upper left corner of each petal, rotating paper to the right until all petals are punched.

In sequence, match corner holes to center hole (pinwheel made). Thread brass fastener through pinwheel and hole in straw and bend ends to hold in place. Blow into the cups of the pinwheel to make it spin. If it will not spin, loosen the brass fastener by making smaller bends in the end. Children can make it spin by waving it in front of them if they cannot blow hard enough.

Closing Routine

--- Notes ---

Winter

Stories Shared

Snowy Day
EZRA JACK KEATS

The Mitten
ALVIN TRESSELT

More Stories to Share at Home

The Red Mittens
LAURA BANNON

Snow on Bear's Nose
JENNIFER BARTOLI

Winter Noisy Book
MARGARET WISE BROWN

Miffy in the Snow
DICK BRUNA

The Snow
JOHN BURNINGHAM

Winter Bear
RUTH CRAFT

Sleepy Bear
LYDIA DABCOVICH

Stopping by the Woods on a Snowy Evening
ROBERT FROST

In the Flaky Frosty Morning
KARLA KUSKIN

I Like Winter
LOIS LENSKI

Henry the Explorer
MARK TAYLOR

Father Fox's Pennyrhymes
CLYDE WATSON

Has Winter Come?
WENDY WATSON

Winter Picnic
ROBERT WELBER

It's Winter
NOEMI WEYGANT

Rhythms, Rhymes, and Fingerplays

Snow

It's snowing! It's snowing!
(wiggle fingers slowly down in front of body)
How the wind does blow.
(blow vigorously)
Snowflakes falling from the sky.
(flutter fingers down again)
One landed on my nose!
(touch nose)

Snowman

Here's a jolly snowman (form chubby tummy with hands)
He has a carrot nose (touch nose)
Along came a bunny (hop)
Looking for some lunch (look around)
He ate that snowman's carrot nose (touch nose)
Nibble (hop), Nibble (hop), Crunch! (sit down)

Five Little Snowmen

Five little snowmen all in a row (hold up five fingers)
Each with a hat (pat top of head)
And a big red bow. (pull at neck like fixing a bow tie)
Out came the sun (arms form big circle over head)
And it stayed all day. (lean to the left)
And one of those snowmen melted away! (put down one finger)

[Repeat with "Four," "Three," "Two," and "One" little snowmen]

Follow-up Ideas

During quiet time look through a photo album and let your toddler identify the people he or she knows. Children like seeing pictures of themselves and acknowledging how much they are growing.

Sliding tubes: Children love to see things go in one end of a cardboard tube and come out the other end. The longer the tube the better! Talk about what will fit in the tube and what is too big for it. Put two things in and see which comes out first.

Mitten matching: Trace your toddler's hands onto a paper sack for a mitten pattern. Cut two mittens from several kinds of materials (paper, cloth, sandpaper, cardboard). Put one of each kind on a table and the others in a paper sack. Have your child pull one mitten from the sack and match it with its mate. This matching game will work with socks, towels, shoes, or any paired items in the home.

Craft

Five Little Snowmen

You will need: white, black, and red felt

scissors

glue

pen or marker

a flannelboard

Draw five snowmen (three circles on top of each other) on the white felt. Make them all different sizes and shapes. Draw five different-sized hats on

the black and bows on the red felt. Cut them out. Turn the pencil marks to the back and assemble each snowman by gluing the hat and bow in place. Draw a face on each one.

Line the snowmen up on the flannelboard or a sofa cushion and recite the "Five Little Snowmen" rhyme. Remove one snowman as each melts. Your child will soon take over the task of "melting" the snowmen. Use the snowmen to talk about size and placement in line: "Let's melt the big one," or "The one in the middle is going to melt next."

Program Notes

Opening Routine	Introduce theme with puppet or toy all bundled up for cold weather with scarf and hat.
Sign	"Snow"—Hold hands high, palms facing down. Wiggle fingers gently as hands slowly fall (like snow falling).
ST	Book: *Snowy Day*
A	"Snow" fingerplay
CD	Re-create actions in the story: dressing warmly, stamping feet, knocking snow off tree onto head, building snowman, making snow angel, putting snowball in pocket.
ST	Display book: *The Mitten.* Flannelboard story using only first five animals and the cricket. (Make mitten in two pieces so that animals can get inside and it can fall apart at the end.)
A	"Snowman" and "Five Little Snowmen" fingerplays
ST	"Five Little Snowmen" flannelboard (see above). Have children continue the sun action from the fingerplay during the rhyme.
QT	Parent and child look at books together
G	Paper snowflakes
	Needed: Lace paper doilies
	Cut into snowflake shapes along the edges.

Closing Routine

┌──────────────── **Notes** ────────────────┐
│   │
│   │
│   │
│   │
│   │
│   │
└──┘

APPENDIXES

Construction of Storytime Materials

There are several items that are used in many, if not all, the programs. The following instructions will assist the storyteller in the construction of these materials.

Lap Stage

Used with puppets and lap board presentations

You Will Need: a cardboard box (at least 10″×13″×16″)

                contact paper, burlap material, or paint

                box cutter

                glue

                Velcro®

                spring clothespins (optional)

Cut the top and back off the box, and cut the two sides as shown in the figure. The remaining whole sides will be the front and floor of the stage.

Cut the sides away from the stage floor as shown. This allows the stage to fold flat for storage or transportation. Glue Velcro strips to the sides and floor to stabilize the lap stage during use. Decorate the stage by painting it or covering it with contact paper or burlap.

To use the stage, set it on your lap with the front facing your audience. Puppets, props, or a script can lay inside on the floor of the stage, easily accessible to you but out of sight of your audience. Finger puppets, rod puppets, or small hand puppets are especially suitable for use with a lap stage.

Scenery can be attached to the stage by gluing it to spring clothespins which are clipped to the top of the stage. A small flannelboard can be attached in the same manner.

The stage can also be used as a lap board (simply turn it around with the floor facing your audience). Standup figures, toys, or props can be manipulated across the stage floor as a story is told.

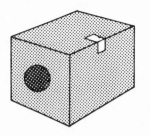

Touchbox

Used for touchbox activities and storage during programs

You Will Need: a cardboard box (all sides intact and a lid that opens)
box cutter
contact paper, material or paint
ribbed top from a sock
glue
straight pins
Velcro® strips

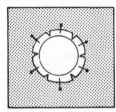

Cut a circular hole in one side of the box, large enough for your hand to easily pass through. Cover the box with contact paper, material, or paint.

Insert one end of the sock-top into the hole, and glue it on the *inside* of the box. Stretch and clip the sock edges to make it fit, and pin the sock in place until the glue dries thoroughly. Remove pins. Glue Velcro to the lid of the box so that it closes securely.

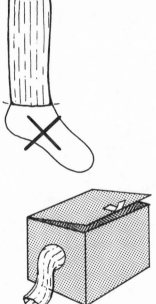

To use, put an object inside the box and close the lid. Demonstrate to the children how your hand can go into the box through the sock. Instruct them to *feel* what is inside the box (but *not* to pull it out through the sock). Encourage them to talk about what they feel: "Is it soft or hard? little or big? warm or cold? Do you know what it is?"

When each child has had a turn, remove the object through the lid of the box. Give them time to see and touch it a second time if they want. Describe the object (color, texture, size, and so on) as they examine it; always name the object (balloon, ball, banana, and so on).

By using the touchbox to keep storytime props, giveaway items, and puppets out of view until they are needed in the program, you make it a familiar part of your storytime. Children will participate more fully in touchbox activities when they see the box often. They like to put things into containers and will readily return storytime props (musical instruments, rod puppets, and so on) to the touchbox when you finish with them.

Generic Glove Puppet

Used with fingerplays and glove puppet stories

You Will Need: a plain cotton gardening glove
Velcro® tabs
needle and thread
pom-poms or felt figures

Sew Velcro tabs to the front and back of each finger tip of the glove. Sew a strip of Velcro to the palm of the glove for scenery or props.

Make figures to use with the glove from pom-poms or felt as shown. Glue a tab of Velcro to the figures so they will adhere to the tabs on the glove.

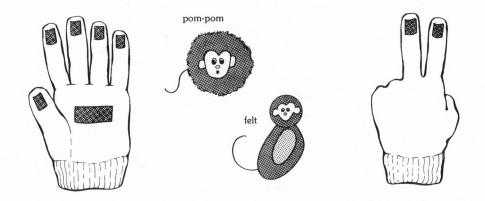

Scenery or props set the stage for a glove puppet story. They can be made from felt or cardboard and attached to the palm of the glove with Velcro.

For counting rhymes, use the Velcro tabs on the back of the glove fingers. Objects can appear or disappear completely as fingers are folded into a fist.

Sock Puppet

Used for tasting fingers and saying goodbye

You Will Need: a knee sock

needle and thread

notions for facial features (buttons, pompoms, yarn)

Place your hand inside the sock with the tips of your fingers near the toe and the heel across your knuckles as shown.

Open your hand wide inside the sock and tuck the toe into the palm of your hand. The mouth is formed. Sew a slot into the bottom of the mouth for your thumb to slide into. This secures the mouth.

Sew on eyes (buttons) keeping them close to the mouth. This makes the puppet less threatening to young children. Add a nose (pompom), hair (yarn) . . . whatever other features or clothing you want to make the puppet special. No teeth, please. Avoid using materials which cannot be washed (like felt). This puppet gets a lot of "loving."

Sock puppets are very flexible and they "make faces" easily. Practice moving your fingers inside the puppet to make it smile, frown, or turn into a silly face.

Practice "talking" in front of a mirror.

To taste fingers, have the puppet ask the children if they want their fingers tasted. If so, the puppet sucks or licks the offered finger with a slurping sound. The puppet then tells each child what his or her finger tasted like. Use flavors with which children are familiar: fruit, soft drinks, dinner items. If children return for additional "tasting," the puppet can oblige but does not need to remember what flavor individuals were. Often the child simply wants to be touched again.

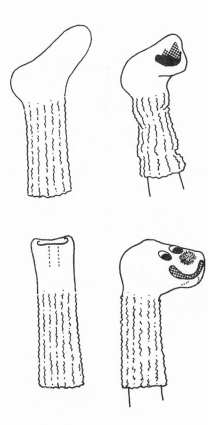

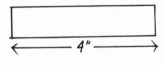

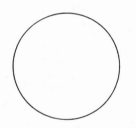

Clown-Shape Puzzle

Used in opening routine

You Will Need: Brightly colored felt in the following shapes:
1 1"×4" rectangle
1 triangle (base 3"; height 4½")
2 circles (1 large, 1 small)
2 small stars
1 crescent (for a smile)

Use basic colors of felt which contrast with each other: yellow, orange or pink, red, purple, blue, green. Toddlers can easily distinguish these colors from each other.

Trace around object like water glasses or salt shakers to obtain patterns for the circles, keeping them in the proportions as shown.

Cut the shapes from felt and place them at random on the flannelboard. As they are rearranged into a clown, name each shape and its relationship to the others. For instance: "This is a triangle. I will put it on top of the big circle . . . put the little circle at the top of the triangle."

As your group becomes familiar with the shapes and their place in the puzzle, put a piece in the wrong place (rectangle at the top of the triangle) and ask them if it looks right. The children will enjoy the surprise and helping you to "get it right."

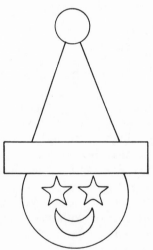

Clown Name Tag

Used to identify children by name

You Will Need: construction paper in basic colors (pink, green, blue, yellow, orange, red, tan, purple)
scissors
glue
gummed stars

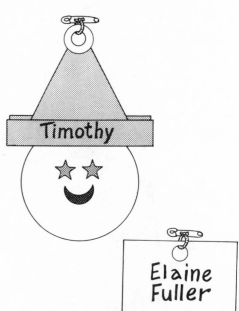

Cut the shapes shown from various colors of construction paper and assemble them into the clown's face. Cut twice as many rectangles as you need. Glue the shapes together, adding the gummed stars as eyes. Glue a second rectangle to the back of each name tag in the same position as the first. Print each child's name on *both* sides of the name tag. Laminate or cover each name tag with clear contact paper.

Punch a hole in the circle pompom and thread with yarn. Use enough yarn to slip the name tag over each child's head or cut it shorter and attach a small safety pin to be pinned to the child's clothing.

Parents' name tags are squares or rectangles of construction paper and have both their first and last names printed on them. Punch a hole in the top and add yarn and a safety pin to attach to the parents' clothing. Keep name tags of child and parent clipped together between programs.

I Know an Old Lady Sack Puppet

Used during the song and for presentation of shapes and colors

You Will Need: 2 grocery sacks

scissors

stapler

tape

8½″×11″ piece of clear acetate (book report cover)

cardboard face, hands, and feet

material scraps

glue

Cut a window (7″×10″) in one sack as shown. Cut a slot under the flap of the sack and another slot along the side fold.

Tape the edges of the window and the slots to reinforce them. Glue the clear acetate on the inside of the sack so that it covers the window.

Insert the second sack into the one with the holes making all corners and edges fit exactly. Staple both sacks across the front just under the window. This keeps the figures from sliding down too far to be seen in the window.

Cover the sack with material, leaving open the slots and window. Glue material securely. Glue on face, hands, and feet.

Insert hand inside of sack so that the fingers make the flap move up and down. When the old lady "swallows" something, flap moves upward and objects are dropped into the slot under it. They then appear in the window. They can be removed through the slot in the sack's side.

For the objects to be swallowed: Make them from felt or heavy posterboard. If felt is used, it must be weighted with fishing or draper weights so that they drop into the window. Posterboard slides down easily.

Create the animals in the song (fly, spider, and so on) and as the song is sung, drop each animal into the window where it can be seen by the children. Also use this puppet to introduce colors, shapes, and alphabet letters. There is no end to the things the Old Lady can eat.

Caterpillar and Butterfly Sock Puppets

Used with *The Very Hungry Caterpillar*

— striped
sock

— white
sock

You Will Need: brightly colored or striped sock

man's white sock, same size as colored sock

a finger from an old glove

felt in the same colors as the sock puppet

glue

buttons and craft eyes

Caterpillar: Insert white sock into colored one. Construct mouth as described in Sock Puppet, sewing through both socks to secure mouth. Add buttons near the mouth for puppet's eyes.

Butterfly: Make and decorate felt wings. Glue craft eyes to the finger from the old glove to make butterfly's body. Glue wings to body.

To use: Fold butterfly's wings over body and flatten. Slide butterfly between white and colored socks. Caterpillar sock puppet stays on the hand for most of story. To spin a cocoon, turn both socks inside out as you pull puppet off hand. Butterfly then emerges from its hidden pocket.

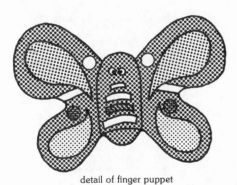

detail of finger puppet

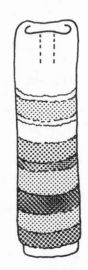

socks inside out

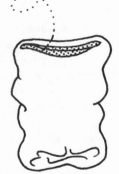

cocoon

How to Read a Picture

"Reading" pictures is the first step toward reading words. It introduces children to vocabulary words and encourages them to use their imaginations and to express feelings and ideas.

Reading pictures acquaints children with books, demonstrating how the story progresses from beginning (front of the book) to end. They also learn that there is a pattern of reading left-to-right as they look at the pages of a book.

Here are some questions you might ask about a picture to encourage discussion with your child:

1. What do you see in the picture? (Children need to know the names of objects as well as people and animals.)
2. What is happening?
3. What are the people (animals) doing?
4. Do you see something funny (sad, silly, dangerous, and so on) in this picture? What do you think will happen next?
5. Do you see someone who is angry (happy, sad, frightened) in this picture? Why do you think he or she is feeling that way?
6. How many ____ do you see? (Children enjoy counting objects in pictures.)
7. What is over (under, beside, behind) the ____ in this picture?
8. I see something that is red (or any color). What do you see that is red in this picture? (or) What color is the boy's shirt?
9. What shapes can you find in this picture? (circles, squares, stars)
10. What do you see that is big? Little?
11. What do you think the girl is saying?
12. What sounds could you hear if you were in this picture? (or) What sound does this cat make?

Reading pictures allows greater flexibility for using books with children of all ages. The story can change with each encounter as new things are discovered in the illustrations. Children become an active part of the story by helping to create it.

BIBLIOGRAPHIES

Program Planning and Storytelling Resources

Anderson, Paul S. *Storytelling for the Flannelboard.* Alhambra, Calif.: Denison, (Book 1) 1963, (Book 2) 1970, (Book 3) 1984.

Association for Library Services to Children. *Opening Doors for Preschool Children and Their Parents.* Chicago, American Library Assn., 1976.

———. *Programming for Very Young Children.* Chicago: American Library Assn., 1980.

Bauer, Caroline Feller. *Celebrations.* New York: Wilson, 1985.

———. *Handbook for Storytellers.* Chicago: American Library Assn., 1977.

———. *This Way to Books.* New York: Wilson, 1983.

Beckman, Carol, et al. *Channels to Children: Early Childhood Activity Guide for Holidays and Seasons.* Colorado Springs, Colo.: Channels to Children Pub., 1982.

Carlson, Bernice W. *Listen and Help Tell the Story.* Nashville: Abingdon, 1965.

Catron, Carol, and Barbara Parks. *Cooking Up a Story with Reproducible Patterns.* Minneapolis: Denison, 1986.

Champlin, Connie. *Puppetry and Creative Dramatics in Storytelling.* Austin: Nancy Renfro Studios, 1980.

———, and Nancy Renfro. *Storytelling with Puppets.* Chicago: American Library Assn., 1980.

Cherry, Clare. *Think of Something Quiet.* Belmont, Calif.: Pitman, 1981.

DeWit, Dorothy. *Children's Faces Looking Up: Program Building for the Storyteller.* Chicago: American Library Assn., 1979.

Elbert, Carol, and Robin Currie. *Rainbows and Ice Cream: Storytimes about Things Kids Like.* Des Moines: Iowa Library Assn., 1983.

Forte, Imogene, and Marge Frank. *Puddles, Wings and Grapevine Swings.* Nashville: Incentive, 1982.

Hunt, Tamara, and Nancy Renfro. *Puppetry in Early Childhood Education.* Austin: Nancy Renfro Studios, 1982.

I Saw a Purple Cow and 100 Other Recipes for Learning. Boston: Little, 1972.

Lima, Carolyn. *A to Zoo: Subject Access to Children's Picture Books.* New York: Bowker, 1982.

Maguire, Jack. *Creative Storytelling: Choosing, Inventing and Sharing Tales for Children.* New York: McGraw-Hill, 1985.

Moore, Vardine. *Pre-School Story Hour.* Metuchen, N.J.: Scarecrow, 1972.

Olson, Margaret J. *Tell and Draw Stories.* Minneapolis: Creative Storytime, 1963.

Pellowski, Anne. *The Story Vine: A Sourcebook of Unusual and Easy-to-Tell Stories from Around the World.* New York: Macmillan, 1984.

Sawyer, Ruth. *The Way of the Storyteller.* New York: Viking, 1962.

Start Early for an Early Start, ed. by Ferne Johnson. Chicago: American Library Assn., 1976.

Taylor, Loren. *Storytelling and Dramatization.* Minneapolis: Burgess, 1965.

Warren, Jean. *Cut and Tell Stories for Fall (Winter and Spring).* Everett, Wash.: Totline Pr., 1984.

Activities and Crafts

Bean, Cheryl A., and Sandra D. Albertson. *Just in Time with Nursery Rhymes.* Longview, Wash.: Just In Time Pub., 1980.

BIG BIRD'S Busy Book, ed. by Sharon Lerner. New York: Random, 1975.

Caney, Steven. *Steven Caney's Playbook.* New York: Workman, 1975.

Chernoff, Goldie. *Easy Costumes You Don't Have to Sew.* Phoenix: Four Winds, 1975.

Cole, Ann, and Carolyn Haas. *Purple Cow to the Rescue.* Boston: Little, 1982.

Frank, Marjorie. *I Can Make a Rainbow: Things to Create and Do for Children and Their Grownup Friends.* Nashville: Incentive, 1976.

Gates, Frieda. *Easy-to-Make Costumes.* Englewood Cliffs, N.J.: Prentice-Hall, 1981.

_____. *Easy-to-Make Puppets.* Englewood Cliffs, N.J.: Prentice-Hall, 1981.

_____. *Glove, Mitten and Sock Puppets.* New York: Walker, 1978.

Hagstrom, Julie. *Let's Pretend: Games of Fantasy for Babies and Young Children.* New York: A & W Visual Library, 1982.

Lopshire, Robert. *How to Make Snop Snappers and Other Fine Things.* New York: Greenwillow, 1977.

Pflug, Betsy. *Funny Bags.* Philadelphia: Lippincott, 1974.

Razzi, James. *Easy Does It!* New York: Parents Magazine Pr., 1969.

Ross, Laura. *Finger Puppets.* New York: Lothrop, 1971.

Supraner, Robyn. *Rainy Day Surprises You Can Make.* Mahwah, N.J.: Troll, 1981.

Nelson, Esther L. *Silly Song Book.* New York: Sterling, 1981.

Nursery Rhymes from Mother Goose in Signed English. Washington, D.C.: Gallaudet College Pr., 1972.

Ohanian, Phyllis. *Songs to Sing with the Very Young.* New York: Random, 1966.

Oldfield, Margaret J. *Finger Puppets and Finger Plays.* Minneapolis: Creative Storytime, 1982.

Poems to Read to the Very Young, comp. by Josette Frank. New York: Random, 1961. (Also *More Poems to Read to the Very Young,* 1968)

Ring a Ring o' Roses: Stories, Games and Fingerplays for Preschool Children. Flint, Mich.: Flint Public Library, 1981.

Tashjian, Virginia. *Juba This and Juba That.* Boston: Little, 1969.

_____. *With a Deep Sea Smile: Story Hour Stretches for Large or Small Groups.* Boston: Little, 1974.

Warren, Jean. *More Piggyback Songs.* Everett, Wash.: Totline Pr., 1984.

_____. *Piggyback Songs: New Songs Sung to Childhood Favorites.* Everett, Wash.: Totline Pr., 1983.

Wirth, Marian, et al. *Musical Games, Fingerplays and Rhythm Activities for Early Childhood.* West Nyack, N.Y.: Parker, 1983.

Wiseman, Ann. *Making Musical Things.* New York: Scribner, 1979.

Fingerplays and Music

Beall, Pamela C., and Susan H. Nipp. *Wee Sing: Children's Songs and Fingerplays.* Los Angeles: Price-Stern, 1980.

Cass-Beggs, Barbara. *Your Baby Needs Music.* New York: St. Martin's, 1978.

Costello, Elaine. *Signing: How to Speak with Your Hands.* New York: Bantam, 1983.

Cromwell, Liz, et al. *Finger Frolics: Fingerplays for Young Children.* Rev. ed. Livonia, Mich.: Partner Pr., 1983.

Glazer, Tom. *Do Your Ears Hang Low? 50 More Musical Fingerplays.* Garden City, N.Y.: Doubleday, 1980.

_____. *Eye Winker, Tom Tinker, Chin Chopper: 50 Musical Fingerplays.* Garden City, N.Y.: Doubleday, 1973.

Grayson, Marion F. *Let's Do Fingerplays.* Washington, D.C.: Robert B. Luce, 1962.

Hart, Jane. *Singing Bee!* New York: Lothrop, 1982.

Kahle, Gratia U. *Favorite Fingerplays and Action Rhymes.* Minneapolis: Denison, 1978.

Keefe, Betty. *Fingerpuppets, Fingerplays and Holidays.* Omaha: Special Literature Pr., 1984.

Langstaff, John. *Jim Along, Josie.* New York: Harcourt, 1970.

My Big Book of Fingerplays: Fun-to-Say, Fun-to-Play, comp. by Daphne Hogstrom. Racine, Wis.: Golden Pr., 1974.

Journal Articles

Baar-Lindsay, Christopher. "Library Programming for Toddlers." *Public Libraries* 22 (1983): 111-13.

Jordan, Anne D., and Jean Mercier. "It's Never Too Early to Start to Read." *Publisher's Weekly,* April 20, 1984, 29-31.

Kewish, Nancy. "South Euclid's Pilot Project for 2-Year-Olds and Parents." *School Library Journal* 25 (1979): 93-98.

Kidstuff: A Treasury of Early Childhood Enrichment Materials. Guidelines Pr., Lake Park, Fla. Published monthly.

McGrath, Nancy. "Early Learning." *Parents Magazine,* October 1980, 66-70.

Markowsky, Juliet K. "Storytime for Toddlers." *School Library Journal* 23 (1977): 28-31.

Smardo, Frances A. "Storyhours Do Make a Difference." *Texas Libraries* 45 (1984): 52-56.

_____. "What Early Childhood Educators Recommend." *Children Today* XX (1980): 25-27.

Totline Newsletter. Totline Pr., P.O. Box 2255, Everett, Wash. Published monthly.

Walsh, Joseph A. "Parenting Programs in Libraries." *School Library Journal* 29 (1983): 32-35.

Weissbourd, Bernice. "As They Grow/Two-Year-Olds." *Parents Magazine.* Regular monthly column.

West of the Moon, "Telling to Toddlers." *Yarnspinner,* Newsletter of the National Assn. for Preservation and Perpetuation of Storytelling, June 1982, 1.

Wortman, B. "Storytime for Two-Year-Olds: Service to the Youngest Patron." *Ohio Library Association Bulletin* 55 (1985): 23–25.

Toddler Characteristics and Parenting Books

Ames, Louise. *Your Two-Year-Old: Terrible or Tender.* New York: Delacorte, 1976.

Aston, Athina. *Toys That Teach Your Child: From Birth to Two.* Charlotte, N.C.: East Woods Pr., 1984.

Bell, T. H. *Your Child's Intellect: A Guide to Home-Based Preschool Education.* Salt Lake City: Olympus, 1972.

Braga, Joseph. *Children and Adults: Activities for Growing Together.* Englewood Cliffs, N.J.: Prentice-Hall, 1976.

Brazleton, T. Berry. *Listen to a Child: Understanding Normal Developmental Problems.* Reading, Mass.: Addison-Wesley, 1984.

_____. *Toddlers and Parents: A Declaration of Independence.* New York: Dell, 1974.

Butler, Dorothy. *Babies Need Books.* New York: Atheneum, 1980.

Crago, Maureen, and Hugo Crago. *Prelude to Literacy: A Preschool Encounter with Picture and Story.* Carbondale: Southern Illinois Univ. Pr., 1983.

Developing Active Readers, ed. by Diane L. Monson and DayAnn McClenathan. Newark, Del.: International Reading Assn., 1979.

Gilbert, Sara. *Three Years to Grow.* New York: Parents Magazine Pr., 1972.

Gordon, Ira. *Baby Learning through Baby Play: A Parent's Guide for the First Two Years.* New York: St. Martin's, 1970.

_____. *Child Learning through Child Play.* New York: St. Martin's, 1972.

Hanstock, Elizabeth. *Teaching Montessori in the Home: The Preschool Years.* New York: Random, 1968.

Holt, John. *How Children Learn.* Rev. ed. New York: Delacorte, 1983.

The Importance of Play (Caring about Kids series). Washington, D.C.: U.S. Dept. of Health & Human Services, 1981.

Larrick, Nancy. *A Parent's Guide to Children's Reading.* 5th ed. Philadelphia: Westminster, 1983.

Levy, Janine. *You and Your Toddler: Sharing the Developing Years.* New York: Pantheon, 1980.

Marzollo, Jean. *Supertot: Creative Learning Activities for Children from 1 to 3.* New York: Harper, 1977.

_____, and Janice Lloyd. *Learning through Play.* New York: Harper, 1972.

Menlove, Coleen. *Ready, Set, Go.* Englewood Cliffs, N.J.: Prentice-Hall, 1978.

Miller, Karen. *Things to Do with Toddlers and Twos.* Marshfield, Mass.: Teleshare, 1984.

Munger, Evelyn M., and Susan Jane Bowden. *New Beyond Peek-a-Boo and Pat-a-Cake: Activities for Baby's First 18 Months.* Piscatawny, N.J.: New Century, 1986.

Neisser, Edith. *Primer for Parents of Preschoolers.* 2nd ed. New York: Parents Magazine Pr., 1972.

Smith, Helen. *Survival Handbook for Preschool Mothers.* Chicago: Follett, 1977.

Stein, Sara, and Children's Television Workshop Staff: *Learn at Home the Sesame Street Way.* New York: Simon & Schuster, 1979.

Taetzch, Sandra. *Preschool Games and Activities.* Belmont, Calif.: Pitman, 1974.

Touw, Kathleen. *Parent Tricks-of-the-Trade.* Washington, D.C.: Acropolis, 1981.

White, Burton. *Parent's Guide to the First Three Years.* Englewood Cliffs, N.J.: Prentice-Hall, 1980.

Titles Used in Programs

Abisch, Roslyn. *Clever Turtle;* illus. by Boche Kaplan. Englewood Cliffs, N.J.: Prentice-Hall, 1969. Frogs

Adams, Adrienne. *Woggle of Witches;* illus. by author. New York: Scribner, 1971. Halloween

Ahlberg, Allan. *Each Peach Pear Plum;* illus. by Janet Ahlberg. New York: Viking, 1978. Peek

Alexander, Ann. *A B C of Cars and Trucks;* illus. by Ninon MacKnight. Garden City, N.Y.: Doubleday, 1956. Vehicles

Alexander, Martha A. *Pigs Say Oink;* illus. by author. New York: Random, 1978. Sounds

Allen, Pamela. *Who Sank the Boat?;* illus. by author. New York: Coward-McCann, 1982. Boats

Anderson, Leone C. *The Wonderful Shrinking Shirt;* illus. by Irene Trivas. Niles, Ill.: Whitman, 1983. Clothing

Aruego, Jose. *Look What I Can Do;* illus. by author. New York: Scribner, 1971. Parades

Asbjornsen, Peter C. *Three Billy Goats Gruff;* illus. by Paul Galdone. New York: Seabury, 1973. Halloween

Asch, Frank. *Just like Daddy;* illus. by author. Englewood Cliffs, N.J.: Prentice-Hall, 1981. Love

_____. *Turtle Tale;* illus. by author. New York: Dial, 1978. Frogs

Balian, Lorna. *Humbug Rabbit;* illus. by author. Nashville: Abingdon, 1974. Rabbits

_____. *Humbug Witch;* illus. by author. Nashville: Abingdon, 1974. Halloween

Bang, Molly. *Ten, Nine, Eight;* illus. by author. New York: Greenwillow, 1983. Bedtime

Bannon, Laura. *The Red Mittens;* illus. by author. Boston: Houghton, 1946. Winter

Barrett, Judi. *Animals Should Definitely Not Wear Clothing;* illus. by Ron Barrett. New York: Atheneum, 1970. Clothing

_____. *I'm Too Small, You're Too Big;* illus. by David Rose. New York: Atheneum, 1981. Sizes

_____. *The Wind Thief;* illus. by Diane Dawson. New York: Atheneum, 1977. Hats

Bartoli, Jennifer. *Snow on Bear's Nose;* illus. by Takeo Ishida. Chicago: Whitman, 1972. Bears and Winter

Barton, Byron. *Airport;* illus. by author. New York: Crowell, 1982. Vehicles

_____. *Buzz, Buzz, Buzz;* illus. by author. New York: Macmillan, 1973. Bugs and Sounds

_____. *Wheels;* illus. by author. New York: Crowell, 1979. Vehicles

Battles, Edith. *What Does the Rooster Say, Yoshio?;* illus. by Toni Hormann. Chicago: Whitman, 1978. Chickens

Berenstain, Stan, and Jan Berenstain. *Bears on Wheels;* illus. by authors. New York: Random, 1969. Vehicles

_____, _____. *He Bear, She Bear;* illus. by authors. New York: Random, 1974. Bears

Beskow, Elsa. *Pelle's New Suit;* illus. by author. New York: Harper, 1929. Clothing

Black, Irma S. *Big Puppy and Little Puppy;* illus. by Theresa Sherman. New York: Holiday, 1960. Sizes

_____. *Is This My Dinner?;* illus. by Rosalind Fry. Chicago: Whitman, 1972. Food and Me

Blevgad, Lenore. *Hark, Hark the Dogs Do Bark, and Other Rhymes about Dogs;* illus. by Erik Blevgad. New York: Atheneum, 1975. Dogs

_____. *Mittens for Kittens and Other Rhymes about Cats;* illus. by Erik Blevgad. New York: Atheneum, 1974. Kittens

Blos, Joan. *Martin's Hats;* illus. by author. New York: Morrow, 1984. Hats

Bonforte, Lisa. *Farm Animals;* illus. by author. New York: Random, 1981. Farms

Booth, Eugene. *In the Air;* illus. by Derek Collard. Milwaukee: Raintree, 1977. Wind

_____. *In the Garden;* illus. by Derek Collard. Milwaukee: Raintree, 1977. Gardens

Bornstein, Ruth. *Little Gorilla;* illus. by author. Boston: Houghton, 1976. Monkeys and Sizes

Boynton, Sandra. *Moo, Baa, La, La, La;* illus. by Kate Klimo. New York: Simon & Schuster, 1982. Sounds

Bram, Elizabeth. *A Dinosaur Is Big.* New York: Greenwillow, 1977. Sizes

Breinbrug, Petronella. *Shawn's Red Bike;* illus. by Errol Lloyd. New York: Crowell, 1975. Vehicles

Bridgman, Elizabeth. *All the Little Bunnies;* illus. by author. New York: Atheneum, 1977. Rabbits

Briggs, Raymond. *Fee Fi Fo Fum;* illus. by author. New York: Coward-McCann, 1964. Sounds

Bright, Robert. *Georgie;* illus. by author. Garden City, N.Y.: Doubleday, 1971. Halloween

_____. *Hurrah for Freddie;* illus. by author. Garden City, N.Y.: Doubleday, 1953. Parades

_____. *My Red Umbrella;* illus. by author. New York: Morrow, 1959. Rain

Brown, Margaret Wise. *Golden Egg Book;* illus. by Leonard Weisgard. New York: Simon & Schuster, 1947. Rabbits

_____. *Goodnight Moon;* illus. by Clement Hurd. New York: Harper, 1947. Bedtime

_____. *Indoor Noisy Book;* illus. by Leonard Weisgard. New York: Harper, 1942. Sounds

_____. *Little Chicken;* illus. by Leonard Weisgard. New York: Harper, 1943. Chickens

_____. *Red Light, Green Light;* illus. by Leonard Weisgard. Garden City, N.Y.: Doubleday, 1944. Colors

_____. *SHHhhh . . . Bang: A Whispering Book;* illus. by Robert De Veyrac. New York: Harper, 1943. Sounds

_____. *Sleepy Little Lion;* illus. by Camilla Koffler. New York: Harper, 1947. Bedtime

_____. *When the Wind Blew;* illus. by Geoffrey Hayes. New York: Harper, 1977. Wind

_____. *Whistle for the Train;* illus. by Leonard Weisgard. Garden City, N.Y.: Doubleday, 1956. Trains

_____. *Winter Noisy Book;* illus. by Charles Green Shaw. New York: Harper, 1947. Winter

Brown, Ruth. *Dark, Dark Tale;* illus. by author. New York: Dial, 1981. Halloween

Bruna, Dick. *B Is for Bear: An ABC;* illus. by author. New York: Methuen, 1972. Bears

_____. *The Fish;* illus. by author. Chicago: Follett, 1963. Food

_____. *I Can Dress Myself;* illus. by author. New York: Methuen, 1977. Clothing

_____. *Miffy in the Snow;* illus. by author. Chicago: Follett, 1970. Winter

_____. *Miffy's Dream;* illus. by author. New York: Methuen, 1979. Rabbits

Brustlein, Janice. *Little Bear Marches in the St. Patrick's Day Parade;* illus. by Marian Foster. New York: Lothrop, 1967. Parades

Bunting, Eve. *St. Patrick's Day in the Morning;* illus. by Jan Brett. Boston: Houghton, 1980. Parades

Burningham, John. *The Baby;* illus. by author. New York: Harper, 1975. Babies

_____. *The Cupboard;* illus. by author. New York: Crowell, 1975. Food

_____. *The Dog;* illus. by author. New York: Crowell, 1975. Dogs

_____. *Mr. Gumpy's Motor Car;* illus. by author. New York: Macmillan, 1975. Rain

_____. *Mr. Gumpy's Outing;* illus. by author. New York: Holt, 1970. Vehicles

_____. *Mr. Gumpy's Outing;* illus. by author. New York: Macmillan, 1971. Boats

_____. *The Rabbit;* illus. by author. New York: Crowell, 1974. Rabbits

_____. *The Snow;* illus. by author. New York: Crowell, 1974. Winter

Burton, Virginia Lee. *Choo Choo;* illus. by author. Boston: Houghton, 1937. Trains

Caldwell, Mary. *Morning, Rabbit, Morning;* illus. by Ann Schweninger. New York: Harper, 1982. Rabbits

Carle, Eric. *Grouchy Ladybug;* illus. by author. New York: Crowell, 1977. Bugs

_____. *Have You Seen My Cat?;* illus. by author. New York: Watts, 1973. Kittens

_____. *1,2,3 to the Zoo;* illus. by author. Cleveland: Collins, 1968. Counting and Trains

_____. *Pancakes, Pancakes;* illus. by author. New York: Knopf, 1970. Food

_____. *The Rooster Who Set Out to See the World;* illus. by author. New York: Watts, 1972. Chickens

_____. *The Secret Birthday Message;* illus. by author. New York: Crowell, 1972. Birthdays

_____. *The Tiny Seed;* illus. by author. New York: Crowell, 1970. Gardens

_____. *The Very Hungry Caterpillar;* illus. by author. Cleveland: Collins, 1970. Bugs and Food

Carrick, Carol. *Rabbit for Easter;* illus. by Donald Carrick. New York: Greenwillow, 1979. Rabbits

Cauley, Lorinda. *Pease Porridge Hot: A Mother Goose Cookbook;* illus. by author. New York: Putnam, 1977. Food

Chandoha, Walter. *Baby Bunny for You;* illus. by author. Cleveland: Collins, 1968. Rabbits

Charles, Donald. *Calico Cat Looks Around;* illus. by author. Chicago: Childrens Pr., 1975. Peek

_____. *Calico Cat's Rainbow;* illus. by author. Chicago: Childrens Pr., 1975. Colors

_____. *Count on Calico Cat;* illus. by author. Chicago: Childrens Pr., 1974. Counting

Chicken Licken; illus. by Jutta Ash. New York: Bradbury, 1972. Chickens

Chorao, Kay. *Baby's Lap Book;* illus. by author. New York: Dutton, 1977. Babies

Chukovsky, Korney. *Good Morning, Chick;* adapted by Mirra Ginsburg and illus. by Byron Barton. New York: Greenwillow, 1980. Chickens

Cleary, Beverly. *Hullabaloo A B C;* illus. by Earl Thollander. Berkeley, Calif.: Parnassus, 1960. Sounds

Coatsworth, Elizabeth. *Good Night;* illus. by Jose Aruego. New York: Macmillan, 1972. Bedtime

Cole, William. *Frances the Face-Maker;* illus. by Tomi Ungerer. Cleveland: Collins, 1963. Me

Collier, Ethel. *I Know a Farm;* illus. by Honore Guilbeau. Reading, Mass.: Addison-Wesley, 1960. Farms

_____. *Who Goes There in My Garden?;* illus. by author. New York: Young Scott Bks., 1963. Gardens

Conover, Chris. *Six Little Ducks;* illus. by author. New York: Crowell, 1976. Ducks

Corey, Dorothy. *You Go Away;* illus. by Caroline Ruben and Lois Axeman. Chicago: Whitman, 1976. Peek

Counting Rhymes; illus. by Corinne Malvern. New York: Simon & Schuster, 1946. Counting

Craft, Ruth. *Winter Bear;* illus. by Erik Blegvad. New York: Atheneum, 1974. Winter

Crews, Donald. *Freight Train;* illus. by author. New York: Greenwillow, 1978. Colors and Trains

_____. *Parade;* illus. by author. New York: Greenwillow, 1983. Parades

_____. *School Bus;* illus. by author. New York: Greenwillow, 1984. Vehicles

_____. *Truck;* illus. by author. New York: Greenwillow, 1980. Vehicles

Cummings, Betty Sue. *Turtle;* illus. by author. New York: Atheneum, 1981. Frogs

Dabcovich, Lydia. *Sleepy Bear;* illus. by author. New York: Dutton, 1982. Bears and Winter

Daughtry, Duanne. *What's Inside?;* illus. by author. New York: Knopf, 1984. Peek

Delaney, Ned. *Bert and Barney;* illus. by author. Boston: Houghton, 1979. Frogs

_____. *One Dragon to Another;* illus. by author. Boston: Houghton, 1976. Bugs

Demarest, Chris. *Benedict Finds a Home;* illus. by author. New York: Lothrop, 1982. Homes

Dennis, Wesley. *Flip and the Cows;* illus. by author. New York: Viking, 1942. Farms

dePaola, Tomie. *Charlie Needs a Cloak;* illus. by author. Englewood Cliffs, N.J.: Prentice-Hall, 1973. Clothing

_____. *The Hunter and the Animals;* illus. by author. New York: Holiday House, 1981. Peek

_____. *Pancakes for Breakfast;* illus. by author. New York: HBJ, 1978. Food

Dunn, Judy. *The Little Duck;* illus. by Phoebe Dunn. New York: Random, 1976. Ducks

Duvoisin, Roger Antoine. *Petunia;* illus. by author. New York: Knopf, 1950. Farms

Eastman, P. D. *Are You My Mother?;* illus. by author. New York: Random, 1960. Love

Ehrlich, Amy. *Everyday Train;* illus. by Martha Alexander. New York: Dial, 1977. Trains

Emberley, Ed. *Birthday Wish;* illus. by author. Boston: Little, 1977. Birthdays

_____. *Drummer Hoff;* illus. by author. Englewood Cliffs, N.J.: Prentice-Hall, 1967. Parades

_____. *Green Says Go;* illus. by author. Boston: Little, 1969. Colors

_____. *The Parade Book;* illus. by author. Boston: Little, 1962. Parades

Erskine, J. M. *Bedtime Story;* illus. by Anne Schweninger. New York: Crown, 1982. Bedtime

Ets, Marie H. *Gilberto and the Wind;* illus. by author. New York: Viking, 1963. Wind

_____. *In the Forest;* illus. by author. New York: Viking, 1944. Parades

_____. *Just Me;* illus. by author. New York: Viking, 1965. Me

Farber, Norma. *Never Say Ugh to a Bug;* illus. by Jose Aruego. New York: Greenwillow, 1979. Bugs

Farmer in the Dell; illus. by Diane Zuromskia. Boston: Little, 1978. Farms

Favorite Best Mother Goose Rhymes; illus. by Richard Scarry. Racine, Wis.: Western, 1976. Vehicles

Fern, Eugene. *Birthday Presents;* illus. by author. New York: Farrar, 1967. Birthdays

Ferro, Beatriz. *Caught in the Rain;* illus. by Michele Sambin. New York: Doubleday, 1978. Rain

Fisher, Leonard E. *Boxes! Boxes!;* illus. by author. New York: Viking, 1985. Peek

Flack, Marjorie. *Angus and the Cat;* illus. by author. Garden City, N.Y.: Doubleday, 1931. Dogs and Kittens

_____. *Angus and the Ducks;* illus. by author. Garden City, N.Y.: Doubleday, 1930. Ducks

_____. *Ask Mr. Bear;* illus. by author. New York: Macmillan, 1932. Birthdays and Love

_____. *Boats on the River;* illus. by author. New York: Viking, 1946. Boats

_____. *Story about Ping;* illus. by Kurt Wiese. New York: Viking, 1933. Ducks

_____. *Wait for William;* illus. by Marjorie Flack and Richard Holberg. Boston: Houghton, 1935. Parades

Fontaine, Jean de la. *The Hare and the Tortoise;* illus. by Brian Wildsmith. New York: Watts, 1966. Frogs

_____. *The Lion and the Rat;* illus. by Brian Wildsmith. New York: Watts, 1963. Sizes

_____. *North Wind and the Sun;* illus. by Brian Wildsmith. New York: Watts, 1964. Wind

Fox, Dorothea. *Follow Me, the Leader;* illus. by author. New York: Parents Magazine Pr., 1968. Parades

Freeman, Don. *Corduroy;* illus. by author. New York: Viking, 1968. Bears

_____. *Dandelion;* illus. by author. New York: Viking, 1964. Rain

_____. *Mop Top;* illus. by author. New York: Viking, 1955. Birthdays

_____. *Pocket for Corduroy;* illus. by author. New York: Viking, 1978. Clothing and Love

_____. *Rainbow of My Own;* illus. by author. New York: Viking, 1966. Colors and Rain

Friskey, Margaret. *Chicken Little Count-to-Ten;* illus. by Katherine Evans. Chicago: Childrens Pr., 1946. Counting

Frost, Robert. *Stopping by the Woods on a Snowy Evening;* illus. by Susan Jeffers. New York: Dutton, 1978. Winter

Funaki, Yasuko. *Baby Owl;* illus. by Shuji Tateishi. New York: Methuen, 1980. Bedtime

Gackenback, Dick. *Claude, the Dog;* illus. by author. New York: Seabury, 1974. Dogs

Gag, Wanda. *Millions of Cats;* illus. by author. New York: Coward-McCann, 1928. Kittens

Galdone, Paul. *The Monkey and the Crocodile;* illus. by author. New York: Seabury, 1969. Monkeys

_____. *The Turtle and the Monkey;* illus. by author. Boston: Clarion, 1983. Frogs and Monkeys

Geisel, Theodor Seuss. *500 Hats of Bartholomew Cubbins;* illus. by Dr. Seuss. New York: Vanguard, 1938. Hats

_____. *In a People House;* illus. by author. New York: Random, 1972. Homes

Gibbons, Gail. *Boat Book;* illus. by author. New York: Holiday House, 1983. Boats

Gingerbread Boy; illus. by Paul Galdone. New York: Seabury, 1975. Food

Ginsburg, Mirra. *Chick and the Duckling;* illus. by Jose Aruego and Ariane Dewey. New York: Macmillan, 1972. Ducks

_____. *Kitten from One to Ten;* illus. by Giulio Maestro. New York: Crown, 1980. Counting

_____. *Mushroom in the Rain;* illus. by Jose Aruego. New York: Macmillan, 1974. Rain

_____. *Three Kittens;* illus. by Giulio Maestro. New York: Crown, 1973. Kittens

_____. *Which Is the Best Place?;* illus. by Roger Duvoisin. New York: Macmillan, 1976. Bedtime

Goodall, John. *Jacko;* illus. by author. New York: HBJ, 1971. Monkeys

_____. *Paddy's New Hat;* illus. by author. New York: Atheneum, 1980. Hats

Grabianski, Janusz. *Cats;* illus. by author. New York: Watts, 1966. Kittens

_____. *Dogs;* illus. by author. New York: Watts, 1968. Dogs

Graham, Margaret B. *Be Nice to Spiders;* illus. by author. New York: Harper, 1967. Bugs

Green, Mary M. *Everybody Has a House and Everybody Eats;* illus. by Louis Klein. New York: Abelard-

Schuman, 1944. Food and Homes

Gregor, Arthur. *One, Two, Three, Four, Five;* illus. by Robert Doisneau. New York: Lippincott, 1956. Counting

Grosvenor, Donna. *Zoo Babies;* illus. by author. Washington, D.C.: National Geographic Soc., 1979. Babies

Hader, Berta, and Elmer Hader. *Cock-a-Doddle-Do;* illus. by authors. New York: Macmillan, 1939. Chickens

Harper, Anita. *How We Live;* illus. by author. New York: Harper, 1977. Homes

Heide, Florence P. *Who Needs Me?;* illus. by Sally Mathews. Minneapolis: Augsburg, 1971. Love

Hewett, Joan. *The Mouse and the Elephant;* illus. by author. Boston: Little, 1977. Sizes

Hill, Eric. *Spot's Birthday Party;* illus. by author. New York: Putnam, 1982. Birthdays

_____. *Spot's First Walk;* illus. by author. New York: Putnam, 1981. Peek

_____. *Up There: A Baby Bear Book;* illus. by author. New York: Random, 1982. Wind

_____. *Where's Spot?;* illus. by author. New York: Putnam, 1980. Dogs

Hoban, Tana. *Big Ones, Little Ones;* illus. by author. New York: Greenwillow, 1976. Sizes

_____. *Dig, Drill, Dump, Fill;* illus. by author. New York: Greenwillow, 1975. Vehicles

_____. *Is It Red? Is It Yellow? Is It Blue?;* illus. by author. New York: Greenwillow. 1978. Colors

_____. *One Little Kitten;* illus. by author. New York: Greenwillow, 1979. Kittens

_____. *Where Is It?;* illus. by author. New York: Macmillan, 1974. Rabbits

Hoberman, Mary Ann. *A House Is a House for Me;* illus. by Betty Fraser. New York: Viking, 1978. Homes

_____. *I Like Old Clothes;* illus. by Jacqueline Chwast. New York: Knopf, 1976. Clothing

_____, and Norman Hoberman. *How Do I Go?;* illus. by authors. Boston: Little, 1958. Vehicles

Holl, Adelaide. *A B C of Cars, Trucks and Machines;* illus. by William Dugan. New York: American Heritage, 1970. Vehicles

Holland, Viki. *We Are Having a Baby;* illus. by author. New York: Scribner, 1977. Babies

Holzenthaler, Jean. *My Feet Do;* illus. by George Ancona. New York: Dutton, 1979. Me

_____. *My Hands Can;* illus. by Nancy Tafuri. New York: Dutton, 1978. Me

The House That Jack Built; illus. by Paul Galdone. New York: McGraw-Hill, 1961. Homes

Hush Little Baby: A Folk Lullaby; illus. by Aliki Brandenberg. Englewood Cliffs, N.J.: Prentice-Hall, 1968. Bedtime

Hutchins, Pat. *Changes, Changes;* illus. by author. New York: Macmillan, 1971. Bugs

_____. *Goodnight Owl;* illus. by author. New York: Macmillan, 1972. Bedtime and Sounds

_____. *Happy Birthday, Sam;* illus. by author. New York: Greenwillow, 1978. Birthdays and Me

_____. *1 Hunter;* illus. by author. New York: Greenwillow, 1982. Counting

_____. *Rosie's Walk;* illus. by author. New York: Macmillan, 1968. Chickens

_____. *Titch;* illus. by author. New York: Macmillan, 1971. Gardens and Me

_____. *The Wind Blew;* illus. by author. New York: Macmillan, 1974. Wind

_____. *You'll Soon Grow into Them, Titch;* illus. by author. New York: Greenwillow, 1983. Sizes

I Know an Old Lady Who Swallowed a Fly: A Folksong; music by Alan Mills, illus. by Nadine Westcott. Boston: Little, 1980. Food

In a Pumpkin Shell: A Mother Goose ABC; illus. by Joan Walsh Anglund. New York: HBJ, 1960. Halloween

Iwamatsu, Jun. *Umbrella;* illus. by author. New York: Viking, 1958. Rain

Jarrell, Mary. *Knee Baby;* illus. by Symeon Shimin. New York: Farrar, 1973. Babies

Jaynes, Ruth. *Benny's Four Hats;* illus. by Harvey Mandlin. Los Angeles: Bowmar, 1967. Hats

Jeffers, Susan. *All the Pretty Horses;* illus. by author. New York: Macmillan, 1974. Bedtime

Jensen, Virginia. *Sara and the Door;* illus. by Ann Strugnell. Reading, Mass.: Addison-Wesley, 1977. Clothing, Homes, and Me

Jewell, Nancy. *Snuggle Bunny;* illus. by Mary Chalmers. New York: Harper, 1972. Love

Jones, Ann. *Holes and Peeks;* illus. by author. New York: Greenwillow, 1984. Peek

Kalan, Robert. *Blue Sea;* illus. by Donald Crews. New York: Greenwillow, 1979. Sizes

_____. *Jump Frog, Jump;* illus. by Byron Barton. New York: Putnam, 1965. Frogs

_____. *Rain;* illus. by Donald Crews. New York: Greenwillow, 1978. Rain

Kauffman, Lois. *What's That Noise?;* illus. by Allan Eitzen. New York: Lothrop, 1965. Sounds

Keats, Ezra Jack. *Jenny's Hat;* illus. by author. New York: Harper, 1966. Hats

_____. *Letter to Amy;* illus. by author. New York: Harper, 1968. Birthdays and Rain

_____. *Peter's Chair;* illus. by author. New York: Harper, 1967. Babies

_____. *Snowy Day;* illus. by author. New York: Viking, 1962. Winter

_____. *Whistle for Willie;* illus. by author. New York: Viking, 1964. Dogs

Kent, Jack. *The Caterpillar and the Polliwog;* illus. by author. Englewood Cliffs, N.J.: Prentice-Hall, 1982. Bugs

_____. *The Egg Book;* illus. by author. New York: Macmillan, 1975. Chickens

Kepes, Juliet. *Five Little Monkey Business;* illus. by author. Boston: Houghton, 1965. Monkeys

_____. *Frogs Merry;* illus. by author. New York: Pantheon, 1961. Frogs

_____. *Ladybird Quickly;* illus. by author. Boston: Little, 1964. Bugs

_____. *Run, Little Monkeys! RUN, RUN, RUN!;* illus. by author. New York: Pantheon, 1974. Monkeys

_____. *The Seed That Peacock Planted;* illus. by author. Boston: Little, 1967. Gardens

Kessler, Ethel. *Big Red Bus;* illus. by Leonard Kessler. Garden City. N.Y.: Doubleday, 1957. Vehicles

_____. *What's Inside the Box?;* illus. by Leonard Kessler. New York: Dodd, 1978. Peek

_____, and Leonard Kessler. *All Aboard the Train;* illus. by authors. Garden City, N.Y.: Doubleday, 1964. Trains

_____, _____. *Do Baby Bears Sit in Chairs?;* illus. by authors. Garden City, N.Y.: Doubleday, 1961. Bears

Knobler, Susan. *The Tadpole and the Frog;* illus. by author. New York: Harvey House, 1974. Frogs

Knotts, Howard C. *Winter Cat;* illus. by author. New York: Harper, 1972. Kittens

Koide, Tan. *May We Sleep Here Tonight?;* illus. by Yasuko Koide. New York: Atheneum, 1981. Bedtime

Koren, Edward. *Behind the Wheel;* illus. by author. New York: Holt, 1972. Vehicles

Kraus, Robert. *Big Brother;* illus. by author. New York: Parents Magazine Pr., 1973. Babies

_____. *I'm a Monkey;* illus. by author. El Cajon, Calif.: Windmill, 1975. Monkeys

_____. *Leo the Late Bloomer;* illus. by Jose Aruego. New York: Dutton, 1971. Me

_____. *Mert the Blurt;* illus. by author. El Cajon, Calif.: Windmill, 1980. Frogs

_____. *Milton the Early Riser;* illus. by author. New York: Dutton, 1972. Bears and Bedtime

Krauss, Ruth. *The Bundle Book;* illus. by Helen Stone. New York: Harper, 1951. Bedtime and Love

_____. *The Carrot Seed;* illus. by David Johnson Leisk. New York: Harper, 1945. Gardens

_____. *Eyes, Nose, Fingers, Toes;* illus. by Elizabeth Schneider. New York: Harper, 1964. Me

Kredenser, Gail. *One Dancing Drum;* illus. by Stanley Mack. New York: S. G. Phillips, 1971. Parades

Kuskin, Karla. *All Sizes of Noises;* illus. by author. New York: Harper, 1962. Sounds

_____. *In the Flaky Frosty Morning;* illus. by author. New York: Harper, 1969. Winter

_____. *James and the Rain;* illus. by author. New York: Harper, 1957. Rain

_____. *Roar and More;* illus. by author. New York: Harper, 1956. Sounds

Kwitz, Mary D. *Little Chick's Story;* illus. by Cyndy Szekeres. New York: Harper, 1978. Chickens

_____. *When It Rains;* illus. by author. Chicago: Follett, 1974. Rain

Lane, Carolyn. *Voices of Greenwillow Pond;* illus. by Wallace Tripp. Boston: Houghton, 1972. Frogs

Lapsley, Susan. *I Am Adopted;* illus. by Michael Charlton. New York: Bradbury, 1974. Babies

Lenski, Lois. *I Like Winter;* illus. by author. New York: Oxford Univ. Pr., 1950. Winter

_____. *The Little Farm;* illus. by author. New York: Oxford Univ. Pr., 1946. Farms

_____. *The Little Sailboat;* illus. by author. New York: Oxford Univ. Pr., 1937. Boats

_____. *The Little Train;* illus. by author. New York: Walck, 1940. Trains

_____. *Surprise for Danny;* illus. by author. New York: Walck, 1947. Birthdays

Lexau, Joan M. *Come Here, Cat;* illus. by Stephen Kellogg. New York: Harper, 1973. Kittens

Lionni, Leo. *Biggest House in the World;* illus. by author. New York: Pantheon, 1968. Homes

_____. *Inch by Inch;* illus. by author. New York: Astor-Honor, 1960. Bugs

_____. *Let's Make Rabbits;* illus. by author. New York: Pantheon, 1982. Rabbits

Little, Jessie J., and Eloise Greenfield. *I Can Do It by Myself;* illus. by Carole Byard. New York: Crowell, 1978. Me

Little Mother Goose; illus. by Jesse Wilcox Smith. New York: Dodd, 1918. Wind

Little Red Hen and the Grain of Wheat; illus. by Paul Galdone. New York: Seabury, 1973. Chickens and Food

Low, Joseph. *Boo to a Goose;* illus. by author. New York: Atheneum, 1975. Farms

Lowrey, Janette S. *Poky Little Puppy;* illus. by Gustaf Tenggren. Racine, Wis.: Golden Pr., 1970. Dogs

Lukesova, Milena. *The Little Girl and the Rain;* illus. by Jan Kudlacek. New York: Holt, 1978. Rain

McCloskey, Robert. *Blueberries for Sal;* illus. by author. New York: Viking, 1948. Bears and Food

_____. *Make Way for Ducklings;* illus. by author. New York: Viking, 1941. Ducks

MacGregor, Ellen. *Theodor Turtle,* illus. by Paul Galdone. New York: McGraw-Hill, 1955. Frogs

Mack, Stanley. *Ten Bears in My Bed: A Goodnight Countdown;* illus. by author. New York: Pantheon, 1974. Bears

Maestro, Betsy. *Wise Monkey Tale;* illus. by Giulio Maestro. New York: Crown, 1975. Monkeys

Marino, Dorothy. *Buzzy Bear in the Garden;* illus. by author. New York: Watts, 1963. Gardens

Martin, Bill. *Brown Bear, Brown Bear, What Do You See?;* illus. by author. New York: Holt, 1983. Colors

Martin, Patricia M. *Jump, Frog, Jump;* illus. by Earl Thollander. New York, Putnam: 1965. Frogs

Martin, Sarah C. *Old Mother Hubbard and Her Dog;* illus. by Paul Galdone. New York: McGraw-Hill, 1960. Dogs

Mayer, Mercer. *A Boy, a Dog and a Frog;* illus. by author. New York: Dial, 1971. Frogs

_____. *Just for You;* illus. by author. Racine, Wis.: Western, 1975. Love

_____. *There's a Nightmare in My Closet;* illus. by author. New York: Dial, 1968. Halloween

Meeks, Esther. *Friendly Farm Animals;* illus. by author. Chicago: Follett, 1956. Farms

_____. *One Is the Engine;* illus. by Joe Rogers. Chicago: Follett, 1972. Trains

Miles, Miska. *Swim Little Duck;* illus. by author. Boston: Little, 1975. Ducks

Miller, Edna. *Mousekin's Golden House;* illus. by author. Englewood Cliffs, N.J.: Prentice-Hall, 1964. Halloween

Mizumura, Kazue. *I See the Winds.* New York: Crowell, 1966. Wind

_____. *If I Were a Mother;* illus. by author. New York: Crowell, 1967. Me

Moreman, Grace E. *No, No Natalie;* illus. by Geoffrey P. Fulton. Chicago: Childrens Pr., 1973. Rabbits

Mother Goose; illus. by Roger Antoine Duvoisin. New York: Heritage, 1943. Rabbits

Mother Goose; illus. by Gustaf Tenggren. Boston: Little, 1940. Trains

Mother Goose; illus. by Gyo Fujikawa. Chicago: Donohue, 1968. Ducks

The Mother Goose Book; illus. by Alice Provenson and Martin Provenson. New York: Random, 1976. Clothing

Mother Goose Nursery Rhymes; illus. by Arthur Rackham. New York: Viking, 1975. Sizes

Mother Goose: 77 Verses; illus. by Tasha Tudor. New York: Oxford Univ. Pr., 1944. Peek

The Mother Goose Treasury; illus. by Raymond Briggs. New York: Coward-McCann, 1966. Bedtime

Mother Goose. *Hurrah, We're Outward Bound;* illus. by Peter Spier. Garden City, N.Y.: Doubleday, 1968. Boats

Mother Goose. *One Misty Moisty Morning;* illus. by Mitchell Miller. New York: Farrar, 1971. Rain

Mother Goose. *1, 2 Buckle My Shoe;* illus. by Gail Haley. Garden City, N.Y.: Doubleday, 1964. Counting

Mother Goose. *Pocketful of Posies;* illus. by Marguerite DeAngeli. Garden City, N.Y.: Doubleday, 1961. Gardens

Mother Goose. *This Little Pig Went to Market: Play Rhymes;* illus. by Margery Gill. New York: Watts, 1967. Me

Mother Goose. *To Market, to Market;* illus. by Peter Spier. Garden City, N.Y.: Doubleday, 1967. Farms

Munari, Bruno. *The Birthday Present;* illus. by author. Cleveland: Collins, 1957. Birthdays

_____. *Who's There? Open the Door;* illus. by author. Cleveland: Collins, 1957. Peek

Murphy, Jill. *Peace at Last;* illus. by author. New York: Dial, 1980. Bedtime

Murphy, Sara. *Animal Hat Shop;* illus. by Mel Pekarsky. Chicago: Follett, 1964. Hats

Nakatani, Chiyoko. *Zoo in My Garden;* illus. by author. New York: Crowell, 1973. Bugs and Gardens

Newberry, Clare T. *Kittens ABC;* illus. by author. New York: Harper, 1965. Kittens

_____. *Marshmallow;* illus. by author. New York: Harper, 1942. Rabbits

Nicoll, Helen. *Meg and Mog;* illus. by Jan Pienkowski. New York: Atheneum, 1972. Halloween

_____. *Meg's Eggs;* illus. by Jan Pienkowski. New York: Harvey House, 1974. Kittens

Noah's Ark; illus. by Peter Spier. Garden City, N.Y.: Doubleday, 1977. Rain

Nodset, Joan L. *Who Took the Farmer's Hat?;* illus. by Fritz Siebel. New York: Harper, 1963. Farms, Hats, and Wind

Oberhansli, Gertrude. *Sleep, Baby, Sleep;* illus. by author. New York: Atheneum, 1967. Babies

Ogle, Lucille. *I Hear;* illus. by Eloise Wilkin. New York: McGraw-Hill, 1971. Sounds

_____. *I Spy with My Little Eye;* illus. by Joe Kaufman. New York: McGraw-Hill, 1970. Peek

Old MacDonald Had a Farm; illus. by Tracey C. Pearson. New York: Dial, 1983. Farms

One I Love, Two I Love, and Other Loving Mother Goose Rhymes; illus. by Nonny Hogrogian. New York: Dutton, 1972. Love

One Rubber Duckie: A Sesame Street Counting Book; illus. by John E. Barrett. New York: Random, 1982. Counting

Over in a Meadow; illus. by Ezra Jack Keats. New York: Scholastic, 1971. Counting

Oxenbury, Helen. *The Birthday Present;* illus. by author. New York: Dial, 1983. Birthdays

_____. *Monkey See, Monkey Do;* illus. by author. New York: Dial, 1982. Monkeys

_____. *Numbers of Things;* illus. by author. New York: Watts, 1968. Counting

Palazzo, Tony. *Animal Babies;* illus. by author. Garden City, N.Y.: Doubleday, 1960. Babies

_____. *Animals 'round the Mulberry Bush;* illus. by author. Garden City, N.Y.: Doubleday, 1958. Monkeys

Peek, Merle. *Roll Over! A Counting Song;* illus. by author. Boston: Houghton, 1981. Counting

Petersham, Maud, and Miska Petersham. *The Box with Red Wheels;* illus. by authors. New York: Macmillan, 1949. Peek

_____, _____. *The Rooster Crows;* illus. by authors. New York: Macmillan, 1939. Chickens

Pfloog, Jan. *Kittens;* illus. by author. New York: Random, 1977. Kittens

_____. *Puppies;* illus. by author. New York: Random, 1979. Dogs

Pienkowski, Jan. *Colors;* illus. by author. New York: Harvey House, 1974. Colors

_____. *Homes;* illus. by author. New York: Messner, 1979. Homes

_____. *Numbers;* illus. by author. New York: Harvey House, 1975. Counting

_____. *Sizes;* illus. by author. New York: Harvey House, 1974. Sizes

Piper, Watty. *The Little Engine That Could;* illus. by George Hauman and Doris Hauman. New York: Platt & Munk, 1961. Trains

Polushkin, Maria. *Morning;* illus. by Bill Morrison. New York: Four Winds, 1983. Sounds

_____. *Who Said Meow?;* illus. by Giulio Maestro. New York: Crown, 1975. Dogs and Sounds

Poulet, Virginia. *Blue Bug Goes to the Library;* illus. by Peggy P. Anderson. Chicago: Childrens Pr., 1979. Bugs

_____. *Blue Bug's Book of Colors;* illus. by Peggy P. Anderson. Chicago: Childrens Pr., 1981. Colors

Prager, Annabelle. *Surprise Party;* illus. by Tomie dePaola. New York: Pantheon, 1977. Birthdays

Preston, Edna M. *One Dark Night;* illus. by Kurt Werth. New York: Viking, 1969. Halloween.

Provensen, Alice, and Martin Provensen. *Our Animal Friends;* illus. by authors. New York: Random, 1974. Farms

Rainbow Mother Goose; illus. by Lili Cassel. Cleveland: Collins, 1947. Colors

The Real Mother Goose; illus. by Blanche F. Wright. Skokie, Ill.: Rand McNally, 1916. Bears

Reiss, John. *Colors;* illus. by author. New York: Bradbury, 1969. Colors

Rey, Margaret. *Curious George Flies a Kite;* illus. by H. A. Rey. Boston: Houghton, 1958. Wind

Rice, Eve. *Benny Bakes a Cake;* illus. by author. New York: Greenwillow, 1981. Birthdays

_____. *Goodnight, Goodnight;* illus. by author. New York: Greenwillow, 1980. Bedtime

_____. *New Blue Shoes;* illus. by author. New York: Macmillan, 1975. Clothing

Rice, Inez. *March Wind;* illus. by Vladimir Bobri. New York: Lothrop, 1957. Wind

Risom, Ole. *I Am a Bunny;* illus. by Richard Scarry. New York: Golden Pr., 1963. Rabbits

Rockwell, Anne F. *Happy Birthday to Me;* illus. by author. New York: Macmillan, 1981. Birthdays

_____. *How My Garden Grew;* illus. by Harlow Rockwell. New York: Macmillan, 1982. Gardens

_____, and Harlow Rockwell. *Toad;* illus. by authors. Garden City, N.Y.: Doubleday, 1972. Frogs

Rockwell, Harlow. *Compost Heap;* illus. by author. Garden City, N.Y.: Doubleday, 1974. Gardens

_____. *I Did It;* illus. by author. New York: Macmillan, 1974. Me

Roffey, Maureen. *Door to Door.* New York: Lothrop, 1980. Homes

Rojankovsky, Feodor S. *Animals on the Farm;* illus. by author. New York: Knopf, 1962. Farms

_____. *Great Big Animal Book;* illus. by author. New York: Simon & Schuster, 1950. Homes

Roy, Ronald. *Three Ducks Went Wandering;* illus. by Paul Galdone. New York: Seabury, 1979. Ducks

Scarry, Richard. *Great Big Air Book;* illus. by author. New York: Random, 1971. Wind

_____. *Hop Aboard! Here We Go!;* illus. by author. Racine, Wis.: Golden, 1972. Vehicles

Schick, Eleanor. *Peggy's New Brother;* illus. by author. New York: Macmillan, 1970. Babies

Schlein, Miriam. *My House;* illus. by Joseph Lasker. Chicago: Whitman, 1971. Homes

Scott, Ann H. *On Mother's Lap;* illus. by Glo Coalson. New York: McGraw-Hill, 1972. Babies and Love

Seeger, Pete. *The Foolish Frog;* illus. by Miloslav Jagr. New York: Macmillan, 1973. Frogs

Sendak, Maurice. *Where the Wild Things Are;* illus. by author. New York: Harper, 1963. Halloween

Seuling, Barbara. *The Teeny-Tiny Woman;* illus. by author. New York: Viking, 1976. Halloween

Shannon, George. *The Surprise;* illus. by Jose Aruego and Ariane Dewey. New York: Greenwillow, 1984. Birthdays

Sharr, Christine. *Homes;* illus. by author. New York: Grosset, 1971. Homes

Shaw, Charles. *It Looked like Split Milk;* illus. by author. New York: Harper, 1947. Peek

Sivulich, Sandra. *I'm Going on a Bear Hunt;* illus. by Glen Rounds. New York: Dutton, 1973. Bears

Skaar, Grace M. *Nothing But Cats and All About Dogs;* illus. by author. Reading, Mass.: Addison-Wesley, 1947. Dogs and Kittens

_____. *Very Little Dog;* illus. by author. Reading, Mass.: Addison-Wesley, 1967. Dogs

_____. *What Do the Animals Say?;* illus. by author. Reading, Mass.: Addison-Wesley, 1968. Sounds

Slobodkina, Esphyr. *Caps for Sale;* illus. by author. Reading, Mass.: Addison-Wesley, 1940. Hats and Monkeys

_____. *Pezzo the Peddler and the Circus Elephant;* illus. by author. Reading, Mass.: Addison-Wesley, 1967. Parades

Smith, Donald. *Farm Numbers 1,2,3;* illus. by author. Nashville: Abingdon, 1970. Farms

Spier, Peter. *Crash! Bang! Boom!;* illus. by author. Garden City, N.Y.: Doubleday, 1972. Parades

_____. *Gobble! Growl! Grunt!;* illus. by author. Garden City, N.Y.: Doubleday, 1971. Sounds

———. *Oh, Were They Ever Happy;* illus. by author. Garden City, N.Y.: Doubleday, 1978. Homes

———. *Peter's Spier's Rain;* illus. by author. Garden City, N.Y.: Doubleday, 1982. Rain

Stein, Sara. *That New Baby;* illus. by Dick Frank. New York: Walker, 1974. Babies

Steiner, Charlotte. *My Bunny Feels Soft;* illus. by author. New York: Knopf, 1958. Rabbits

———. *My Slippers Are Red;* illus. by author. New York: Knopf, 1957. Colors

Stewart, Robert. *The Daddy Book;* illus. by Don Madden. New York: American Heritage, 1972. Love

Suba, Suzanne. *The Monkeys and the Pedlar;* illus. by author. New York: Viking, 1970. Monkeys

Tafuri, Nancy. *Have You Seen My Duckling?;* illus. by author. New York: Greenwillow, 1984. Ducks

Tall Book of Mother Goose; illus. by Feodor Rojankovsky. New York: Harper, 1942. Birthdays

Taylor, Mark. *Henry the Castaway;* illus. by author. New York: Atheneum, 1972. Boats

———. *Henry the Explorer;* illus. by Graham C. Booth. New York: Atheneum, 1966. Winter

———. *Time for Flowers;* illus. by Graham C. Booth. Pasadena: Ritchie, 1967. Gardens

Thomas, Anthony. *Things We See;* illus. by G. W. Hales. New York: Watts, 1976. Peek

The Three Bears; illus. by Paul Galdone. New York: Seabury, 1972. Bears

Tolstoy, Aleksei. *The Great Big Enormous Turnip;* illus. by Helen Oxenbury. New York: Watts, 1968. Gardens, Sizes, and Food

Towend, Jack. *Railroad A B C;* illus. by Eenison Budd. New York: Watts, 1944. Trains

Tresselt, Alvin. *Autumn Harvest;* illus. by Roger Antoine Duvoisin. New York: Lothrop, 1951. Food

———. *Follow the Wind;* illus. by Roger Antoine Duvoisin. New York: Lothrop, 1953. Wind

———. *The Mitten;* illus. by Yaroslava S. Mills. New York: Lothrop, 1964. Winter

———. *Rain Drop Splash;* illus. by Leonard Weisgard. New York: Lothrop, 1946. Rain

———. *Wake Up, Farm!;* illus. by Roger Antoine Duvoisin. New York: Lothrop, 1957. Farms

Waber, Bernard. *Ira Sleeps Over;* illus. by author. Boston: Houghton, 1972. Bedtime

Wahl, Jan. *Pleasant Fieldmouse's Halloween Party;* illus. by Wallace Tripp. New York: Putnam, 1974. Halloween

Watanabe, Shigeo. *How Do I Put It On?;* illus. by author. New York: Philomel, 1979. Me and Clothing

Watson, Clyde. *Catch Me, Kiss Me, Say It Again;* illus. by Wendy Watson. Cleveland: Collins, 1978. Love

———. *Father Fox's Pennyrhymes;* illus. by Wendy Watson. New York: Crowell, 1971. Winter

Watson, Wendy. *Has Winter Come?;* illus. by author. Cleveland: Collins, 1978. Winter

Weelen, Guy. *Little Red Train;* illus. by Mamoru Funai. New York: Lothrop, 1966. Trains

Weiss, Harvey. *My Closet Full of Hats;* illus. by author. New York: Abelard-Schuman, 1962. Hats

Welber, Robert. *The Winter Picnic;* illus. by Deborah Ray. New York: Pantheon, 1970. Food and Winter

Welch, Martha M. *Will That Wake Mother?;* illus. by author. New York: Dodd, 1982. Kittens

Wells, Rosemary. *Max's New Suit;* illus. by author. New York: Dial, 1979. Clothing and Rabbits

———. *Max's Toys, a Counting Book;* illus. by author. New York: Dial, 1979. Counting

Westerberger, Christine. *The Cap That Mother Made;* illus. by author. Englewood Cliffs, N.J.: Prentice-Hall, 1977. Hats

Weygant, Noemi. *It's Winter;* illus. by author. Philadelphia: Westminster, 1969. Winter

Wildsmith, Brian. *The Lazy Bear;* illus. by author. New York: Watts, 1974. Bears

———. *Little Wood Duck;* illus. by author. New York: Watts, 1972. Ducks

Wilkin, Eloise B. *Ladybug, Ladybug and Other Nursery Rhymes;* illus. by author. New York: Random, 1979. Bugs

Williams, Garth. *The Chicken Book;* illus. by author. New York: Delacorte, 1970. Chickens and Counting

Wolde, Gunilla. *Betsy and the Vacuum Cleaner;* illus. by author. New York: Random, 1979. Me

———. *Betsy's Baby Brother;* illus. by author. New York: Random, 1974. Babies

Wondriska, William. *Puff;* illus. by author. New York: Pantheon, 1960. Trains

Wood, Audrey. *The Napping House;* illus. by Don Wood. New York: HBJ, 1984. Bedtime

Wood, Kay. *Grover's Favorite Color;* illus. by author. New York: Children's Television Workshop, 1977. Colors

Woolley, Catherine. *I Like Trains:* illus. by George Fonseca. New York: Harper, 1965. Trains

Young, Miriam. *If I Drove a Tractor;* illus. by Robert Quackenbush. New York: Lothrop, 1973. Farms

———. *If I Drove a Train;* illus. by Robert Quackenbush. New York: Lothrop, 1972. Trains

———. *If I Flew a Plane;* illus. by Robert Quackenbush. New York: Lothrop, 1970. Vehicles

———. *If I Sailed a Boat;* illus. by Robert Quackenbush. New York: Lothrop, 1971. Boats

Zaffo, George J. *Giant Nursery Book of Things That Go;* illus. by author. Garden City, N.Y.: Doubleday, 1959. Vehicles

Zindel, Paul. *I Love My Mother;* illus. by John Melo. New York: Harper, 1975. Love

Ziner, Feenie. *Counting Carnival;* illus. by Paul Galdone. New York: Coward, 1962. Parades

Zion, Gene. *Harry, the Dirty Dog;* illus. by Margaret B. Graham. New York: Harper, 1956. Dogs

———. *No Roses for Harry;* illus. by Margaret B. Graham.

New York: Harper, 1958. Clothing

Zolotow, Charlotte. *Hold My Hand;* illus. by Thomas di Grazia. New York: Harper, 1972. Love

_____. *In My Garden;* illus. by Roger Antoine Duvoisin. New York: Lothrop, 1960. Gardens

_____. *Mr. Rabbit and the Lovely Present;* illus. by Maurice Sendak. New York: Harper, 1962. Rabbits and Colors

_____. *When the Wind Stops;* illus. by Howard Clayton Knotts. New York: Abelard-Schuman, 1962. Wind

Index to Program Themes

Judy Nichols is a free-lance professional storyteller and puppeteer now living in Sedgwick, Kansas. She was previously a children's librarian in the Decatur (Ill.) Public Library, the Wichita (Kan.) Public Library, and the Elkhart (Ind.) Public Library. Nichols is a member of Puppeteers of America and the National Association for the Preservation and Perpetuation of Storytelling.